Shapeshifting
FOR LAW ENFORCEMENT CNT/HNT

Ellis Amdur, M.A., N.C.C., C.M.H.S.
Ret. Sgt. Lisbeth Eddy

Effective Scenario Training for
Crisis / Hostage Negotiation Teams

An Edgework Book
www.edgework.info

Notes and Notices

SHAPESHIFTING FOR LAW ENFORCEMENT CNT/HNT: Effective Scenario Training for Crisis / Hostage Negotiation Teams

By Ellis Amdur, M.A., N.C.C., C.M.H.S. and Lisbeth Eddy © 2015

ISBN: 978-0-9985224-6-3

A Message to Our Readers

Edgework is committed to offering the best of what our years of experience and study have taught us. We ask that you express your respect for these intentions and honor our work by adhering strictly to the copyright protection notice you will find below. Please know that by choosing NOT to reproduce these materials, you are supporting our work and making it possible for us to continue to develop materials that will enhance both officer and public safety. We thank you sincerely for your vigilance in respecting our rights!

Credits
Design: Soundview Design Studio
Cover photograph: Ellis Amdur

Contents

Published Works by Ellis Amdur (and Co-Authors)

Published by Edgework www.edgework.info

On the De-escalation of Aggression, Hostage Negotiation and Psychology

BODY AND SOUL: Toward a Radical Intersubjectivity in Psychotherapy – Ellis Amdur

COOLING THE FLAMES: Communication, Control, and De-escalation of Mentally Ill & Aggressive Patients
A Comprehensive Guidebook for Emergency Medical Services – Ellis Amdur & John K. Murphy

EVERYTHING ON THE LINE: Calming and De-escalation of Aggressive & Mentally Ill Individuals on the Phone
A Comprehensive Guidebook for Emergency Dispatch (9-1-1) Centers – Ellis Amdur

FROM CHAOS TO COMPLIANCE: Communication, Control, and De-escalation of Mentally Ill, Emotionally Disturbed & Aggressive Offenders
A Comprehensive Guidebook for Parole and Probation Officers – Ellis Amdur & Alan Pelton

GUARDING THE GATES: Calming, Control and De-escalation of Mentally Ill, Emotionally Disturbed & Aggressive Individuals
A Comprehensive Guidebook for Security Guards – Ellis Amdur & William Cooper

GRACE UNDER FIRE: Skills to Calm and De-escalate Aggressive & Mentally Ill Individuals in Outpatient Settings: 2nd Edition
A Comprehensive Guidebook for Those in Social Services or Helping Professions – Ellis Amdur

IN THE EYE OF THE HURRICANE: Skills to Calm and De-escalate Aggressive & Mentally Ill Family Members: 2nd Edition – Ellis Amdur

SAFE BEHIND BARS: Communication, Control, and De-escalation of Mentally Ill & Aggressive Inmates
A Comprehensive Guidebook for Correctional Officers in Jail Settings – Ellis Amdur, Michael Blake & Chris De Villeneuve

SAFE HAVEN: Skills to Calm and De-escalate Aggressive & Mentally Ill Individuals: 2nd Edition
A Comprehensive Guidebook for Personnel Working in Hospital and Residential Settings – Ellis Amdur

SAFETY AT WORK: Skills to Calm and De-escalate Aggressive & Mentally Ill Individuals
A Comprehensive Guidebook for Corporate Security Managers, Human Resources Staff, Loss Prevention Specialists, Executive Protection, and Others Involved in Threat Management Professions – Ellis Amdur & William Cooper

SHAPESHIFTING for Law Enforcement CNT/HNT: Effective Scenario Training for Crisis/Hostage Negotiation Teams – Ellis Amdur & Ret. Sgt. Lisbeth Eddy

THE COORDINATOR: Managing High-Risk High-Consequence Social Interactions in an Unfamiliar Environment – Ellis Amdur & Robert Hubal

THE THIN BLUE LIFELINE: Verbal De-escalation of Mentally Ill & Emotionally Disturbed People
A Comprehensive Guidebook for Law Enforcement Officers – Ellis Amdur & John Hutchings

THREAT DE-ESCALATION: How to Effectively Assess and Diffuse Dangerous Situations (Book & DVD)
A Publication of the United States Concealed Carry Association – Ellis Amdur

Published by Freelance Academy Press www.freelanceacademypress.com

DUELING WITH OSENSEI: Grappling with the Myth of the Warrior Sage – *Revised & Expanded Edition* – Ellis Amdur

HIDDEN IN PLAIN SIGHT: Tracing the Roots of Ueshiba Morihei's Power – *Revised & Expanded Edition* – Ellis Amdur

OLD SCHOOL: Essays on Japanese Martial Traditions – *2nd Expanded Edition* – Ellis Amdur

Fiction

Published by Jet City Comics

THE CIMARRONIN: A Samurai in New Spain: *A Graphic Novel* – Neal Stephenson, Charles Mann, Ellis Amdur & Mark Teppo

Published by Edgework Books

THE GIRL WITH THE FACE OF THE MOON – Ellis Amdur

Published Works by Lisbeth Eddy

CRIMINAL PSYCHOLOGY, Jacqueline B. Helfgott, PhD, Editor. **Volume Three: Implications for Forensic Assessment, Policing and the Courts—Chapter 7,** Eddy, Lis, "The Elements of Hostage (Crisis) Negotiation" Praeger Press, Santa Barbara, California, 2013

In Gratitude for Expert Critique

The following professionals have closely reviewed this book. With each draft, we corrected errors of fact, added new information, and fine-tuned the manuscript. One of the qualities of a good law enforcement officer is the understanding that the task supersedes protecting someone's feelings: therefore, we have appreciated all the direct criticism.

All responsibility for this book, however, must lie in our hands. Any errors, in particular, are ours alone. Given lives are on the line in work such as this, please do not hesitate to contact us if you believe any part of this book is inaccurate or needs additional material. We will revise the book, as needed, in future editions. Our thanks to:

Sergeant Jessica Crowley is a 21 year veteran for the Village of Bartlett Police Department in Illinois where she is a patrol sergeant serving as a shift supervisor and Coordinator of the Bartlett Crisis Intervention Team. She is the Northern Illinois Co-Coordinator for the Illinois State Training Board's Crisis Intervention Team 40 hour Curriculum and trains police officers on Co-Occurring Disorders. Sergeant Crowley is a Hostage Negotiator, a member of the Northern Illinois Critical Incident Stress Debriefing Team (NICISM) and CIT International. She holds a Masters in Human Resource Management, and is a graduate of both Northwestern University School of Staff and Command and the Suburban Law Enforcement Academy Managerial and Leadership.

Retired Sergeant James Detrick is a retired sergeant of the Auburn Police Department, Auburn, Washington. He has thirty-five years of law enforcement training experience, is a trained hostage/crisis negotiator, mental health first aid instructor, and assists with the Crisis Intervention Training program in King County, Washington.

Sergeant Matthew Onderbeke has been a law enforcement sheriff's deputy for 32 years, including 28 years in patrol, one year as a detective and 4 years as an evidence control supervisor. He has served as a Field Training Officer and a Field Training Officer Instructor for the State of Washington, and is a past Vice Director of the Washington State Chapter of the National Association of Field Training Officers. Sergeant Onderbeke has been a member of his agency's SWAT Negotiator Unit for approximately 22 years, and has also attended the Crisis Negotiators Course at the Canadian Police College, Ottawa, Ontario Canada. He has attended many negotiator-training conferences across the United States and Canada, and has presented at three conferences, and has also attended SWAT Supervisors Management Training. He received training in suicide intervention from the Volunteers of America, and volunteered on that organization's intervention chat-line. Sergeant Onderbeke has been a member of the Western States Hostage Negotiators' Association for 22 years, has served as a district representative and secretary/treasurer for the association, and has represented the association at the National Council of Negotiation Associations. He is currently the president of the Western States Hostage Negotiator's Association.

Deputy Aaron Walker has eighteen years of law enforcement experience. Deputy Walker started his career for a rural Sheriff's Office in southwest Missouri, where he along with other deputies, started that agency's first SWAT team. In 2005, he transferred to the city where he was hired as the Assistant Chief, later becoming the Chief. In 2009, he moved to North Idaho, where he works as a patrol deputy with the Bonner County Sheriff's Office. Here he is assigned to the Hostage/Crisis Negotiation Team, Dive Team, Taser Instructor, Field Training Officer, CIT Coordinator, and C.I.T. Instructor. Deputy Walker also volunteers as an Advanced EMT.

I

Foreword

Crisis negotiation—of which hostage negotiation is a subset—is one of the most remarkable areas of law enforcement.[1] Through a combination of tactical communication, empathic connection and, at times, subterfuge, negotiators persuade desperate, suicidal or homicidal individuals, often intoxicated or mentally ill, to relinquish their position of power and submit to police authority. Not all barricaded or static situations, however, are truly negotiable. A perpetrator of an act of mayhem may merely desire an audience to his or her crime, or someone to keep him or her company before executing a suicidal act. In other cases, their actions are attempts to draw first responders into a position of vulnerability so that they can enact either a 'suicide by cop' or an ambush. In all such cases, the negotiator serves a vital function: by focusing the subject's attention upon his or her voice, this gives the tactical officers—SWAT[2] —time and position to directly intervene to stop the crime in process.

The Role Player

Crisis negotiation requires a high level of skill. This can only be developed through practice. Such practice also gives a team leader the opportunity to assess his or her negotiators, to assure their abilities remain at peak levels, and also pick out weak points in their repertoire. First-rate training, however, is not easy. Consider the maxim: "As you practice, so you will do." In this light, training must conform closely to real crises. This requires realistic role-play, something easier said than done. Such training has a number of requirements:

- The role-play must be true to life. This means it must conform to the way people truly act in such crises. A role player must, therefore, either have an understanding of crisis negotiation, or be coached *during* the scenario by a 'shadow' who is in the room with the role-player. Hostage takers as well as victim takers, tend to follow—and negotiators definitely *must* follow—certain patterns of behavior that differ from what the uninitiated might assume from watching movies or reading novels;
- The role-play should be true to the behaviors of a person in that particular crisis;
- Additionally, the role-play must be true to the behaviors a person suffering from a mental disorder would genuinely display in such a situation;
- As the role-play is set up for the purpose of improving skills, the training exercise should end in success. 'Table-top' or other informal training exercises can be repeated over and over until it is

---

[1] The authors will refer to negotiators either as "crisis negotiators" or HNT

[2] The authors are aware of a number of other names for specialty units besides SWAT (Special Weapons and Tactics). Among them are such terms as SRT (Special Reaction Team), SOG (Special Operations Group), ERT (Emergency Response Team) ERU (Emergency Response Unit) and TU (Tactical Unit). In order that the text is readable, we have chosen the term SWAT, perhaps the most commonly used acronym. This does not indicate our preference for this term over any other.

done perfectly, but it would certainly be counter-productive were the department invest in the expense to set up a full training exercise, only to have it aborted or terminated in the first half hour when the hostage-taker 'kills' the hostage. The role player, therefore, in cooperation with the team leader, must monitor the exchange he or she is having with the lead negotiator, and at times, give *in-character* cues when the negotiator is off-target. For example, if the negotiator is talking too much, or trying to tell the subject what to do, rather than practicing tactical paraphrasing, the subject should yell, "You are not listening!" followed, perhaps, by hanging up the phone;

- Sometimes, when necessary, the subject will demand a new negotiator. This is for the purpose of keeping the exercise going when the initial negotiator has lost his or her way. It can also be deliberately programmed into the scenario so more than one negotiator can use the opportunity to practice. However, another aspect that should be built into practice is a manipulative subject, or one who is so unorganized they cannot focus on either progress or a positive outcome. When *they* demand a change of negotiators, this is a good opportunity for the team to practice refusing their demands in a way that doesn't flame the subject up

- The only exception to 'building in success' would be if the negotiating team is so incompetent or lackadaisical that they need a hard wake-up call. In such a case, the hostages should be killed or the subject kills himself or herself to underscore the deadly seriousness of the training. At this point, there should be an immediate after-action review, and the exercise can be restarted or closed down, whichever would make the team stronger.

All in all, this is a tall order. You will need someone who is not only familiar with the behaviors of desperate, drug affected, and/or mentally unstable individuals. They also need to be someone who is familiar with crisis negotiation *and* is a good actor. Given a negotiation team is usually a small entity within a department with a variety of competing demands on limited funds, most departments cannot hire such a professional on a regular basis. Furthermore, once used, could the professional actor be used again? His or her voice would be familiar, and he or she will have participated in the debriefing, thereby establishing a personal relationship with the team. Familiarity may hopefully not breed contempt, but it also takes away the edge that makes the training exercise feel real. Because training should be a regular rather than one-time occurrence, professional trainers should be a rarity rather than the norm.

Who, then, should be a role player? One option is to use acting students, or amateur actors from a local theater company. One can also use people known to the negotiation team who are both teachable and have acting talent. In any event, they must be educated in several things:
- The purpose of scenario training
- The requirement to follow the direction of the 'shadow coach'
- They should be assessed in a short audition to ascertain if they can simultaneously think on their feet, follow directions and not go 'off message,' because they imagine they know what a hostage taker would do.

Another option is to use police officers. The authors believe law enforcement officers who are part of the same team are rarely suitable as role-players. Team members recognize their voice and style of interaction on both sides of the role-play, and with such familiarity, it is very hard to make things realistic. Even the use of officers from another agency can be problematic. There is a tendency among all too many officers to become overly competitive with the team and break character or lose sight of the exercise. Another flaw can be that the officer second-guesses the team's strategies, based on his or her beliefs on how s/he personally would interact with such a subject. To be sure, the use of officers from another agency, unfamiliar to the team, can be successful, but the aforementioned factors must be taken into account by both the organizers of the training exercise and the role-player.

The Scenarios

The reader will find in the following pages thirty different training scenarios. They are colorful, unpredictable, and multi-layered. Just as a real situation can change radically when new information is brought in, most of the scenarios will have unexpected twists requiring the negotiators to think on their feet and sometimes diametrically change directions.

Many of the scenarios can be programmed in two ways: for a successful negotiated scenario or an impasse. In the latter case, failure is deliberately architected, so negotiators can learn to recognize a situation gone bad, and SWAT is given a chance to practice their skills for which they have mustered.

Using this book, a team should be able to orient role-players on how the team wants the training to go. You will have scenario training that you can make as realistic as possible. Each scenario has instructions on best practice communication strategies for someone displaying the particular type of disturbed behavior highlighted in the scenario. The role-player and coach, if used, are both informed of these strategies. The role-player responds positively when the team uses them, and negatively when they do not. There are three ways to use these strategic communication tactics:
  • The team is instructed in the strategies. The exercise is agenda-driven so specific skills are honed and practiced to pattern them as part of one's repertoire. Think of this as a 'table-talk' exercise;
  • They are used by a psychological consultant, or members of the team act as 'runners' who hypothetically received information from a consultant, mid-exercise, to drive the exercise forward towards a successful conclusion;
  • The team is NOT informed of such strategies. It's sink or swim. At the end of the exercise, be it successful or not, these strategies are brought up in an after-action review, as a comparison with what the team actually tried.

We have tried to give role-play scenarios covering the gamut of mental illness and personality disorders, as well as common crises that lead otherwise ordinary people into desperation.
  • It is quite easy to rework a scenario based on your own specific training needs and resources. You can, of course, change gender, age, race, etc. of the role players: just be sure to write out a script with the changes. In such a case, our scenario can serve as a template, where the scenario

functions as a guide to the type of personality the role-player must assume, even though specific details are changed. If you decide to change ethnic or cultural details, consult with a subject matter expert in the culture you are concerned with, showing them the scenario. You may find something that is a dilemma in one culture may not be a major problem in another. For example, consider Scenario 12, where you have a young teenager from Pakistan, suicidal because she is being forced into marriage. Should you change this to a young Japanese national, she is more likely, in modern times, to be suicidal because she believes she disappointed and shamed her parents in failing academically or in a job situation. In essence, you can use the same scenario as a core template to make alternative scenarios for a number of training exercises, each time focusing on cultural and religious issues that may drive a crisis situation.

- The team-leader can also 'pare' down the complexity of the situation, particularly when working with a new team, or when time is limited, feeding the team the information in increments, making the 'role-play' to be an 'educational exercise,' rather than a true-to-life scenario.

Training Procedure

The team leader gives the initial information—who, what, where—to the team, once everything is staged (Of course, the organizer of the exercise will not reveal the title of the scenario, which would give the team members too much of a 'lead' in the negotiation).

Further information is acquired in the same way Intel is gathered in real situations. Preferably, the team leader should recruit persons to act as 'interviewees' for the Intel-gathering members of the team to work with. Depending on the way the scenario is set up, (and how many actors/participants the team leader has available); additional role players (family, friends, professionals) pass on the information exactly as would happen in real life, through secondary interviews. In this way, the secondary members of the team get a chance to practice their interview skills. The secondary interviewees can be coached on how to make the interview challenging in a realistic way. If the secondary interviewers are ineffective, they will NOT receive necessary information from the interviewees. In cases where secondary interviewees are not available:

- The team leader (or coordinator of the training i.e. the "director"), can pass out envelopes containing the appropriate background material, etc. This information should only be given out if the team member asks the right questions of the coordinator of the training exercise, and explains to him or her who they would interview and what information they are looking for.
- If there is an assistant team leader, he or she becomes the 'information person' and takes on the role of each person the Intel gatherers would wish to interview. They don't have to act the part, but would merely provide information when the proper questions and requests are posed. For example, a team member states they would try to interview a next-door neighbor. The information person would state whether the neighbor was or was not available. If available, they would provide information to appropriate inquiries. If the Intel gatherer states they understand the subject has a sister who lives in San Francisco, and would like to interview her, the information person would ask how they intend to locate her. Once the Intel officer describes a reasonable

way to find and contact that person, the information person 'becomes' that sister and answer questions accordingly, thus providing the necessary information. This removes the need for an additional role-player, and reduces the need for the preparation of all the written Intel to be done ahead of time. It also allows for some flexibility in problem solving for the Intel negotiators when figuring out how to go about finding and retrieving information.

The scenario, as written out in the book, is NOT passed to the team as a cheat sheet. We have had critical readers object that the scenarios are 'too complex.' <u>That complexity is for the role player, so that he or she can actually build a character.</u> Furthermore, it gives the 'director', usually the team leader, suitable opportunities to introduce other characters who can be debriefed by the team.

Scenarios Within the Corrections Environment

This book primarily focuses upon law enforcement negotiations. We have offered two scenarios involving the corrections environment. Many smaller detention facilities—jails, in particular—do not have dedicated negotiation teams, who must be called from outside to respond to hostage crises (because of the particular environment, barricade subject situations are far less likely to require HNT-type interventions). We therefore wished to offer police teams an opportunity to practice for situations where they might be called to a detention facility. The authors have also written a companion volume *Shapeshifting for Correctional Facility CNT/HNT: Effective Scenario Training for Crisis/Hostage Negotiation Teams.*

SWAT's Role Within the Training Scenario

Effective Coordination Between HNT and SWAT

One of the biggest problems that occurs in 'barricade subject' situations of any type, much less hostage situations, is poor coordination and communication between SWAT and HNT. These two divisions must practice together so that flaws in communication as well as development of a clear chain of command are highlighted and addressed. The writers are aware of far too many situations where HNT and SWAT inadvertently function in opposition to each other or when SWAT is not aware of what progress (or lack thereof) HNT has made with the barricaded subject.

HNT and SWAT must function together as a 'meta-team.' Problems of coordination, communication and command should be ironed out during training, not in the field while an incident is in progress.

If SWAT is part of the exercise, the exercise should be deliberately crafted and role-player instructed for eventual 'failure' so the SWAT team does not simply stage for hours without anything to do. That said, boredom and stasis are realistically part of the tactical team's job description, and teams that have not honed the ability to tolerate boredom may sometimes act in ways that are not tactically sound.

If possible, various 'exercises' for the SWAT team should be developed for them to actually practice. SWAT can practice food deliveries, release of an injured hostage, delivery of the throw phone, or documents the subject has demanded. They can plant listening devices, or attempt to get a visual on the scene. As said earlier, team leaders can program the negotiation exercise for failure, something that SWAT will not be informed. When it is suddenly time to go, they must be ready to tactically respond.

And, keep in mind, as the SWAT team develops ideas, it's certainly useful for them to practice them, even if those ideas are never put to use in the particular scenario. For example, as unique and special needs come up in a given situation, there might be a requirement for SWAT to practice and become familiar with equipment they have never used before. Quite possibly, a situation could resolve itself in many different ways before SWAT has the need to actually execute the plan as developed. (In 1997, Seattle Police had a stand off with a man armed with a samurai sword in downtown Seattle. The situation took 11 hours to resolve. Ultimately, it was resolved using fire hoses and a ladder. The SWAT team had to practice for many hours with equipment they borrowed from Seattle Fire, before executing the plan that took this man safely into custody).

The trainer may be creative, enacting a scenario with SWAT intervention, and then, later, 'picking up' at that point, essentially having a second round as a 'do-over.' However, done this way, the exercise does lose an element of adrenaline. It is our sense that the 'do-over' should follow a *successful* negotiation. The negotiation team and role-player should 'rewind' approximately ½ hour to one hour (time for a second negotiator to practice), but this time the role-player should escalate into a negative situation, enabling SWAT to fully practice their skills.

Some of these scenarios may seem rather outlandish. However, life is truly more bizarre and savage than fiction. Each scenario is based on real incidents and real people, the majority of whom the authors have actually encountered.

Essential Information on Communication with Emotionally Disturbed Subjects

This book assumes that the reader has already acquired basic knowledge of emotionally and disturbed individuals as their behaviors pertain to law enforcement or corrections. Whatever the reader's level of knowledge in this area, comprehensive basic information can be acquired through:

- **THE THIN BLUE LIFELINE:** Verbal De-escalation of Mentally Ill and Emotionally Disturbed People – *A Comprehensive Guidebook for Law Enforcement Officers* by Ellis Amdur & John Hutchings
- **SAFE BEHIND BARS:** Communication, Control, and De-escalation of Mentally Ill and Aggressive Inmates – *A Comprehensive Guidebook for Correctional Officers in Jail Settings* by Ellis Amdur, Michael Blake & Chris De Villeneuve
- **THE COORDINATOR:** Managing High-Risk High-Consequence Social Interactions in an Unfamiliar Environment by Ellis Amdur

All of these books, as well as a future companion volume, **SAFE WITHIN THE WALLS:** Communication, Control, and De-escalation of Mentally Ill and Aggressive Inmates – *A Comprehensive Guidebook for Correctional Officers in Prison Settings* can be acquired at www.edgeworkbooks.com

SCENE COMMANDER

HNT Team Leader

- Sergeant or senior team member
- Liaison with scene commander and SWAT
- Coordinates written sit-rep
- Monitors stress level of HNT members
- Plans for relief, if necessary
- Determines selection of positions and changes, if necessary

SWAT

- Tactical response

Primary

- Communicates with subject
- Not anyone of rank
- Distraction free (should be isolated except secondary and team leader
- No promises made
- No agreements without consult

Secondary (coach)

- Controls access to primary
- Monitors negotiation and provides feedback and ideas
- Is a second ear
- Watches primary's stress level

Intel (likely more than one officer)

- Gathers ALL info on subject
- Interviews family, friends, doctors, mental health providers, etc.
- Runs records checks and computer searches
- Provides relief for other positions

Scribe (recorder)

- Keeps written time line
- Documents everything
- Provides notes for primary and secondary
- Hangs posters, etc.

NOTE: This should be regarded as a general model.
Details will vary depending such factors as your organizational structure, available resources and the size of your team.

II

A Note on Psychological Consultation

Best practice demands a negotiation team has a psychological consultant. Mental health professionals (psychiatrist, psychologist, and counselor) almost never participate in direct negotiation. A police crisis negotiator must be prepared, in certain situations, to abet in the killing of the hostage taker. Few mental health professionals, by training, experience, or disposition, are suited for this. A psychologist-negotiator may find himself/herself in an ethical dilemma, known as a 'dual relationship,' where his/her professional responsibility to offer therapeutic interventions may conflict with the negotiator role, which may require misdirection, manipulation, distraction, even lying to the hostage taker in order to ensure the safety of the victims.

This principle is not ironclad. There are teams who use mental health professional/non-police personnel in direct negotiations, but this is justifiably rare. In any event, all negotiators *must* go through standard negotiation training, and furthermore, we strongly recommend all non-law enforcement personnel associated with a crisis negotiation team should go through a civilian police academy, defensive tactics training and also engage in "ride-alongs' to gain some understanding of actual police work and culture (or in the case of jails/prisons, that of correctional officers). In particular, they should experience some simulated training in 'shoot/no-shoot' decision-making, using SIRT® pistols or Simunitions®. There are strict protocols that have been learned through bitter experience. You should never have a non-law enforcement negotiator learning protocols on the job, particularly police procedure.

The more usual role for the mental health professional is as a consultant: listening in on the conversation, and trying to get a handle on the psychological organization or disorganization of the hostage taker or barricaded subject, or responding to a phone call off-site, and offering informed suggestions on how best to carry out the negotiations.

Hopefully, the team leader, typically a sergeant, has already developed credibility with the command staff, and, if fortunate, with the SWAT team. Having a mental health professional on scene to back up the negotiations team's requests/suggestions/assessment will allow them to be considered more seriously by the command staff.

In terms of training scenarios, the mental health professional can provide a vital role in setting up a role play, and in particular, teaching the role player how to understand the subject he or she is playing from the 'inside out.' Based on extensive experience with that 'type' of person, the consultant can give cues on how to talk, and literally how to move (physical organization—body language that mirrors the behaviors of people suffering from a particular illness or mindset—is the best avenue to effective role playing, just as it is in acting). In some scenarios, the mental health professional works as part of the team doing the negotiation. In other trainings, he or she can be in the room with the role-player, coaching them so they stay true to the character and scenario.

The mental health professional must have some humility here. If he or she does not have *direct* experience with the type of individual in a particular role-play, he or she should assist the department in securing a consultant with that knowledge. This can often be done without incurring costs—for example, let us imagine a role play with a teenaged hostage taker, where the negotiation team avails itself of a child mental health specialist from the local mental health agency, thereby ensuring the young actor stays true to character. This can be used as an opportunity for mental health agencies to increase their level of collaboration with their local law enforcement agency. This is particularly important for both agencies, because many misdemeanant arrests involve mentally ill individuals, and services during and after release from custody are essential. A good relationship between your two entities, fostered by mutual consultation and aid, will be invaluable.

How to Effectively Use Psychological Consultation in the Training Exercises

Some teams start with a psychological consultant on scene and others bring on the consultant only in more complicated cases. You should, of course, follow your standard operating procedures.

- If you start with a consultant, he or she should go into the scenario 'cold,' just like the officers, and offer consultation as he or she usually does. After an hour or two, the consultant should look at the 'consultation' in the book, and use it to augment his or her own advice.
- If you only use a consultant when cases get complicated, or you call 'outside' for help when needed, treat the 'consultation' in the text as if it were a simulated call to a consultant

In general, you can either have your psych consultant use the material, adding their own suggestions, or you can read it, as if it was sent by email from consultants far away. If you wish to challenge a member of the team, have someone read it to the team member on the phone, as if from a consultant. The team member must take good notes and report what s/he learned to the rest of the team. Any data not accurately reported will not be available to the team. This will be discussed during the after-action review.

III

How to Set Up the Role Play

1. The scenario can be set up from simple to elaborate, depending on personnel and resources. The authors have participated in some excellent role-play that involved no more than two rooms, and a phone in the same building. Other, more complicated training scenarios have entailed taking over a fire station while armed with a sword, holding three hostages in sub-freezing weather in an abandoned apartment building (trading two hostages for hot soup!), providing consultation in the middle of a forest while sitting in an armored personnel carrier, and holding hostages in a factory booby-trapped by the SWAT team leader so his team could meticulously practice safely going through a huge, dark, unknown environment without getting blown up.

2. Decide if this will be a 'negotiating team alone' exercise, or will include SWAT. If it is going to include SWAT participation, it is important to have a representative from the SWAT team participate in development and implementation of the training exercise, so that their team's time is well spent.

3. Decide on the goals for both teams: Will they be programmed in beforehand to hone specific training objectives, or will it be open-ended?

4. Pick the scenario you want your team to work on. Either the team leader (or if he or she wants to participate in the exercise, another team member) is the director.

5. Role-play (fictitious) information can be inserted into department records so that support staff, when asked, can 'pull up' criminal history and other records which thereby make Intel gathering more realistic.

6. Provide the role-player with the scenario. Have them go over the character with the psych consultant or director (if the latter is familiar enough with the personality type), and rehearse with him or her, including having them move like such a person might move. They need to get into character.

7. The information in the psych consult in each chapter can be used to help coach the role player how to play the part. However, do not simply give it to him or her to read, as they will, unavoidably, start tracking the strategies used for de-escalation. Rather, instruct them on the relevant aspects of the subject's behavior, motive and psychological make-up, much like a film director would to an actor, and help them, thereby, get in character.

8. The director should clearly explain the objectives of the exercise. Teach the role player what are effective strategies that will be used by the hostage negotiator, such as active listening. Particularly with a role-player new to negotiation, either the director or an assistant (someone who is very familiar with hostage negotiations) will be present in the barricaded individual's location to coach the person so they do not do or say something unrealistic to disrupt the training exercise.

You may have to coach (whisper) responses congruent with how barricaded subjects respond to maintain realism. This 'shadow coach' needs to be somehow identified as not being 'in play,' usually by wearing a traffic vest or something of that nature. Whatever 'identifier' is chosen, it must be consistent with all personnel who need to be moving about in the scenario who are NOT in play. It is important to keep these numbers of personnel to an ABSOLUTE minimum. They are 'invisible' to the negotiation team or SWAT, if they are listening:

9. If space is limited, because of the location/venue of the 'incident', such as in a vehicle, a two-way radio can be used to communicate and direct the role player. There are some limitations to this, as whoever is doing the directing needs to be able to follow both sides of the conversation, and really stay on top of things:

10. How to respond when the negotiator is 'off track':
   - If the negotiator is talking at the subject and neither listening nor 'lining up' with them, the subject will go into a tirade, yelling, "You are not listening!" They may hang up the phone;
   - If the negotiator says something stupid, which the actor might not realize, the coach will tell the role-player how to react;
   - When the role-player needs a break they can cut off the call in a variety of ways. They can use statements like, "I'm sick of you" to "I'm hungry. I'm going to eat something. Call me later;"
   - If the team is not taking the exercise seriously, (this happens, on occasion), the role-player should be instructed to kill himself/herself or the hostage. Then the team gets the privilege of the sharp edge of the team-leader's tongue.[3]
   - The coach will help the role-player bargain for things—anything from something that is do-able, food for example, to a police escort to the airport—so that the negotiators can practice gaining concessions, taking control incrementally, tiring the subject out, etc;
   - If this is not a hostage situation, but rather a 'victim taking,' the negotiator should practice communicating with the subject, engendering enough interest/connection so that they stay on the line, enabling the SWAT team to get into a tactical position to neutralize them.

11. If the exercise is time-limited, the coach will be essential in assisting the role-player to realistically, pace concessions, the development of rapport, etc.

---

[3] This illustrates one more advantage of regular practices around volunteer role players. With no unnatural pressure to draw things out due to the money expended when securing professional services, the team, easily enough, can try again in a few weeks, or as mentioned earlier, 'reboot' in some fashion while still on scene.

IV

Essential Principles—Make It Personal

One hallmark of crisis situations is we forget the obvious. The crisis negotiator is striving to establish a connection with the hostage/victim taker or barricaded subject. In different ways, a hostage taker and a victim taker are in an apocalyptic situation. The hostage taker cannot conceive of any better way out of his or her crisis than taking someone prisoner. The victim taker wants to create his or her own personal apocalypse, but they either want a witness (you) while they do it, they still need to amp themselves up further or, unconsciously, they are looking for a way out. The barricaded subject sees contact with the officers as a threat. In all cases, the connection you are striving to establish is human. Such a connection immediately establishes that the individual in crisis is no longer isolated. S/he has someone working *with* him or her. When an individual no longer feels alone, new ideas, including hope, arise and they are, at best, willing to surrender power to the law enforcement officers, or at minimum, divided in their intentions (part of them wanting to surrender and part of them still wanting to cause harm). In the latter case, an individual with divided intentions loses situational awareness and may, therefore, be easier to neutralize if that is required.

You cannot establish a connection with an individual unless they perceive you as human. Therefore, as expeditiously as possible, introduce yourself. (There are several viewpoints on this: some negotiators introduce themselves with their first name; others with their title and the department for whom they work). Outline, in the most general sense, what you are trying to do in talking with them. In crisis negotiation, human connection is the ultimate tactic. Without it, no other tactic will have any power at all.

V

Essential Principles: Tactical Paraphrasing—A Reminder

"I don't need good talkers. I need good listeners"
—Sgt Don Gulla, King County Crisis Negotiation Team

Paraphrasing is perhaps the most important technique in crisis negotiation, particularly in the early stages. As many times as we have worked with negotiation teams, and as often we have seen this emphasized, all too many negotiators neglect to use this strategy effectively.

Tactical paraphrasing is NOT repeating what the other person has said, or even summarizing, in your own words, what they said. Rather, you inform the subject, with a phrase or sentence, your UNDER-STANDING of what they said. If you paraphrase effectively, you have established that you have 'gotten it' that far, so they don't have to repeat themselves, or try to say it in other words. It is like peeling off a single layer of an onion so you can be shown the next one. If you don't show you 'get it,' the hostage taker or barricaded subject will get frustrated, and feel forced to repeat and/or elaborate that layer of the problem with more and more intensity. As the situation gets more intense, they usually get more irrational, and their ability to communicate breaks down even further. The wonderful thing about paraphrasing is you don't have to be 'smart' and interpret anything. You simply have to listen carefully.

Returning to our image of an onion, as you peel off each layer, the hostage taker/barricaded subject reveals the next layer of whatever is driving them. They might start out complaining about so many police outside the building. You paraphrase by saying, "You don't want those guys around." Then, they begin to tell you their wife left, and you paraphrase, "What a lousy day. You had no idea your wife would leave, and things get so bad, all of a sudden police are outside your house," and then the subject starts talking about suicide.

Paraphrasing establishes you're truly listening and have understood what they have said. An additional component of tactical paraphrasing is where we also take a slightly activist approach. We select what we will paraphrase, subtly steering them in the direction of safety.

This method is 'self-correcting,' whereas passive reflection can make things worse. If you sum up an angry person's worst impulses, they may find themselves in full agreement with you. Here is an example of an incorrect response. "Seeing the police outside makes you want to cut off her head." You have lined up with the part of them that desires destruction! However, if you sum up an aspect of what they have said in the direction of conflict resolution, you will draw out of them that which desires a favorable outcome. On the other hand, if they're, in fact, bent on mayhem, they will correct you by escalating what they're saying, believing you aren't getting the message. <u>Remember, they're trying to communicate, or they wouldn't be talking to you.</u>

Example of self-correction:

Police – "You didn't want it to come to this. You've been hoping you could simply talk this through peacefully."

Subject – "No, you don't get it. I don't want to 'talk this through.' I wanted her right where I got her, sitting here, unable to move, while I tell her how much I hate her guts. When I'm finished with that, we'll see what happens next."

Why not simply ask the hostage taker/barricaded subject what's going on? If they want to tell you, won't they just answer your questions? Asking too many questions is usually not a good idea with really angry people. They already believe you have to understand what they're saying, and a question shows that you don't. (That's why you hear such angry demands as "Don't you get it?" or "How many times do I have to say the same thing?" or "Suppose I spell this out for you slow enough for even you to comprehend." Or even, "If I cut off one of his ears, will you get it now?") Furthermore, they may perceive your questions as an interrogation, of you trying to take control. The subject, particularly if angry, can easily view your questions as a 'power grab,' and will often escalate to take back control.

Of course, there are some basic questions one asks right at the beginning, such as "Are you alright?" or "Is anybody hurt?" Beyond that, and particularly if they are not forthcoming with answers, tactical paraphrasing helps get communication going, focuses the hostage taker on you rather than the victim(s), often fixes their position, and gives them a sense that someone is hearing them out.

How to Use Paraphrasing Successfully

- It is very important that your voice is calm and strong. You speak to the individual as someone who has the power within to take care of both himself and his problem, not as someone who is fragile or volatile . . .even if he is.
- Contact the strong aspect of the individual, the future looking side, which is striving for a resolution to the situation rather than an apocalypse. If you 'support' the weak or the insecure aspects of the person, you may foster regression to a less mature level of action. Childish action is often impulsive or violent.
- Sometimes, you can use a dramatic summation, "You're really ticked off!" Here, you sum up the individual's mood with your voice, in addition to what is being said.

Using Paraphrasing to Communicate with Individuals with Severe Mental Illness

Paraphrasing can be remarkably effective for communication with severely mentally ill individuals. Given the internal chaos people experience when psychotic, manic, drug intoxicated (a time-limited, externally-induced mental illness), or disorganized, it is essential we don't add to their sense of confusion by barraging them with questions or attempting to solve their problems by taking over and telling them what they should feel or do. When the mentally ill person gets confused, losing track of what he was saying, or drifts off into a tangent, just paraphrase the last thing they said. This will help them reorient to the subject of concern.

Core Level within Paraphrasing

We know we have reached the core level when there is no more 'progress.' The person spins his wheels. They may use different words, but they say essentially the same thing over and over again. Some express relief at being finally understood. Some exhibit an intensification of emotion, because you have reached that which is most distressing. When you reach the core, and it is clear you' have truly established rapport, you can begin problem-solving. This can be:

- Further paraphrasing, where you show greater and greater understanding about what they're upset about;
- A summation of the core problem, followed by a puzzled "why?" For example, "You trusted him, and let him stay in your home. He came on to your daughter and stole money. I can understand why you'd be so furious at him. What I'm confused about is this: if you shoot him, he wins. He's hurt or dead, sure, but you will go to prison, and there will be no one home to protect your daughter from the next man like him. We have to figure out a way you can win so you will still be there when your daughter needs you next time."
- With some individuals, you have, by paraphrasing them every step of the way, established that you're a person of trust. In some cases, you can now be quite directive, because people are often willing to accept advice or even instruction from those they trust;
- With others, we're ready to engage in a collaborative process of problem-solving, trying to figure out a way to solve the situation in the best interest of everyone involved.

How to Efficiently Develop Skills in Paraphrasing

Outside of realistic scenario training, many find it hard to practice paraphrasing in a manner that does not seem utterly contrived. Taking five minutes at every 'shift change' to practice paraphrasing is simply not going to happen, and won't be effective anyway. Furthermore, if you view paraphrasing as a 'specialized,' pseudo-counseling technique, you probably won't want to do it—and you won't be good at it anyway. When you are hit by adrenaline, dealing with an angry, perhaps mentally deranged individual, you will stumble over your words if you try to speak 'psychologese,' saying things like:

- "So what you are sharing with me is . . ."
- "What I hear you saying is . . ."

Don't do this! Many subjects will find you irritating, and you will be trying to speak in a way that you never talk like in daily life. You must be absolutely present to what is going on right now, not 'stuck in your head,' trying to say things in the 'right' way.

You are, in fact, a master of paraphrasing. You do it all the time simply keeping a conversation going, saying things like:

- "Your kid flunked out, huh?"
- "You're not getting a raise."
- "You hate that guy."
- "She's the one."

In short, the natural statements you intersperse in any conversation are perfect paraphrasing. However, because you do this unconsciously, it's hard to tap into as an *emergency technique*. You need to make this a conscious skill, something that's easy to perfect. Consider this—how many conversations do you have a day? Twenty? Thirty? Forty? In each and every conversation, at an arbitrary moment of your choosing, decide to paraphrase the next thing they say. <u>Only one statement</u>. For example, your friend says: "I'm thinking of going hunting this weekend." You, instead of asking a question, say, "You got your license already," or "You want to get an elk again this year, huh?" Here's another example: your friend says, "My daughter got on the honor role. Finally." You reply, "Her grades really went up this quarter, didn't they," or "You've been waiting a long time." Then, whatever the response, you go back to your conversation in your usual manner.

Your conversational partner won't even notice. But because you made a conscious decision to do this, your brain notices. That means you have practiced that skill twenty to forty times a day. Consider how good your shooting skills would be if you do twenty, thirty, forty perfect shots a day—it would become automatic! Similarly, if you do this every day, you will be able to step into crisis oriented paraphrasing without hesitation. It will be so natural to you that you do not even have to think about it.

VI

Don't Forget the Value of Scenario Training to Hone the Skills of Potential 'Coaches' or 'Secondary Negotiators.'

When debriefing true hostage negotiation/barricaded subject incidents, most all eyes are on the primary negotiator. The primary is the position most (if not all) HNT members aspire to become. All HNT members are waiting for their turn in the 'hot seat.' This is where the action is, and most consider it the most important position on the team. Nonetheless, all members will concede that crisis negotiation is a team effort. Successful outcomes would not be as common without the efforts of the Intel people, and the other team members helping out in the background, not to mention the presence and security that SWAT provides.

In all actuality, the most important member of the team is probably the 'secondary' or 'coach' negotiator. This position is usually occupied by one of the most skilled team members. This member is in a position where the adrenaline is running a little lower than for the primary. This enables the coach to see things with a broader view, thereby processing the information through a different filter. This coach is not only involved in the processing of the information and development of the negotiation strategies, but is also tasked with keeping an eye on the primary negotiator. There have been incidents where the primary has become too emotionally involved with the subject, and has inadvertently tipped them off as to developing SWAT actions. In other cases, primaries have become so close to the subject, that they lose their objectivity when discussing possible outcomes. The coach has the responsibility to ensure the primary does not go astray with regard to their feelings for the subject (either positive or negative). If the coach sees this issue developing, it is their responsibility to bring it to the attention of the team leader, who can discuss it with the primary, and secondary, and a decision can be made as to whether or not to switch negotiators.

The coach truly is a critical role. Scenario-based training provides the team leader/director with an opportunity to watch to see how different members can perform in this role. This is not a role that comes naturally to most negotiators, and just because one is very experienced in the field does not necessarily mean they will perform well as a coach.

Some of the very best negotiators are very poor coaches. When placed into the role of coach, they cannot help but take over. Instead of 'coaching' the primary by listening and providing suggestions as needed, they begin to feed the primary lines, one at a time, as if the primary had no idea what to say. This can be very annoying, and also does not let the team leader assess the skills of the person who is acting as primary for the training.

On the other hand, some 'coaches' may not participate at all. Instead, they sit with a set of headphones on, neither engaging in strategy sessions nor paying attention to what they need to.

The role of the secondary is a difficult role to fill. As stated before, most negotiators would rather be 'doing it themselves' than observe and help. It takes a very disciplined negotiator to fulfill this role. Scenario-based training is a good time to find who can do so when needed. The best coach is one who can listen, guide and direct an inexperienced or new negotiator through an exercise. That way, the new negotiator gains some skill and confidence by learning from one of the veterans. The coach can also provide a different kind of guidance when a negotiator, even a veteran, begins to lose focus and the situation goes sideways.

Built-In Secondary Negotiator Training

The team leader can deliberately create a training scenario, in collaboration with the primary, where the latter develops too strong of rapport with the subject, interfering with the process. This challenges the coach to step up and do something about it, and enables the team leader to observe how the rest of the team reacts. Having to make decisions about changing negotiators is something the team needs to be comfortable with; furthermore, all must understand that there can be no arguments when/if the time comes. If good reasons are provided, the changes need to be made, so the process can continue.

VII

Texting

The authors recently heard about an excellent training exercise by Snohomish County, Washington Sheriff's Office that was carried out entirely through texting. A bright young teenager was recruited and oriented towards a suicidal situation. She was simply asked to reflect on some of her friends that have had trouble with parents, bullying or the like and to construct the character as the training went along. She was also coached by the director on how hostage negotiation works, and how it should be resolved. Because of the technological challenge, the director decided to do a straightforward negotiation, rather than a complex one. Texting was more than enough of a challenge!

There are two circumstances where texting/communication is likely to occur:
- A hostage is surreptitiously communicating with the police (or texting a friend, who communicates in turn with law enforcement). In this case, the communication will likely be in brief, short bursts.
- A subject communicates directly. The negotiators were really challenged! They didn't understand the various emoticons and slang, and they were too slow with their thumbs. The young person was often confused by the negotiator's response, because he was six or seven texts behind what the kid was saying.

Because texting is becoming almost ubiquitous, it is an essential skill that at least several team members should be expert. Like touch-typing, the expert 'texter' thumbs words at an amazing rate of speed. Your texting specialist should familiarize himself/herself with various emoticons and abbreviations. They must go on line frequently to find out what the new slang is.

While the "text-negotiation" is taking place, a secondary should be ready, logged into Google or Bing, so they can instantly type various incomprehensible-to-the-negotiator abbreviations, so they can signal the negotiator what each of them means.

On texting scenarios

We have not set up a specific scenario drill here for text negotiations or hostage communication, but as described above, it should be easy to integrate into a training exercise.

VIII

On Scenario Training

**This chapter—and only this chapter—is copied and given as a handout
to the team before the training exercise.**

Important

This training is for educational purposes. This includes not only the negotiating team, but also all the observers. The role player will be presenting a character encompassing specific behaviors associated with mental disorder/personality disorder/substance abuse, etc. Within the designated time period, our intention will be to allow both observers and participants to experience what interacting with someone of this style might be like. This includes recognizing some of the signs and symptoms, trying out various interventions, and experiencing some of your reactions, the negative ones in particular, that someone of this style might engender.

Be Aware

At various times, the subject may hang up the phone:
- Because it's what the person would do in the situation;
- To indicate, clearly, that the negotiator is off-course;
- So the supervisor of the exercise is able to use the time to pass new info to the team or to bring in new role players, such as family members or escaped hostages for collateral interview practice. The collateral subjects may need to be de-escalated themselves: escaped hostages and family members are often very agitated, showing everything from hysterical fear to anger at the negotiating team.

Possible Outcomes & Situations
- An interaction will take place throughout the time period, with no resolution. Progress will be made, and we will debrief what worked well, or what might have worked better, etc.
- A resolution truly occurs and the hostage taker surrenders.
- The situation is going somewhat badly, and will likely get worse. Ensuring the exercise continue, rather than it ending in disaster, the role player may get very belligerent, and demand another negotiator. The role player will probably hang up the phone. If such a situation occurs, the team should discuss if the situation is really going poorly. If so, both in the interests of continuing the exercise, and also increasing the learning process, we sometimes recommend changing negotiators. Otherwise, the hostages might be killed. On the other hand, the demand for another negotiator may be just a power play. Thus, you have to be aware of the connection/control you

have or do not have with the hostage taker, because the latter situation requires you continue and do not change. The former, however, allows the role player and supervising observers to signal a potentially fatal situation without completely aborting the exercise.

- The situation goes badly, for whatever reason, and the hostage is in danger. Tactical forces are called in and the hostage taker is neutralized.

Guarantees

- The role player will make this an educational exercise.
- No attempt will be made to 'cheat', to make the scenario a no-win situation, or to shame the team. This does not include the difficult, perhaps obnoxious behaviors typical of the type of hostage taker we are training to deal with.
- Whoever the role player is, they will have the humility to be directed in how to play the role by the team leader, and when included, a psychological consultant. They will be 100% willing to accept direction throughout, so the training exercise makes the team and individual members stronger. Everyone is training for life-and-death events, so scenario training will be treated that way.

SCENARIO 1

Bipolar Disorder

1 – Original Call

Complainant states an 11 year old neighbor boy came to her house, claiming his father had his mother tied up in a chair, and was pointing a gun in her face. Officers responded, and surrounded the house. After attempts to contact the father were unsuccessful, they requested SWAT and HNT.

1 – Interview with Child

Joseph Garamond is a 32-year-old male, a husband and father of one son. Eleven-year-old Jamey had been playing at a friend's house, and came home to find his father acting very strangely. He has been increasingly irritable for several months, stays up late ("my mom tells him to come to bed, and he says he's never tired. He says he doesn't need to sleep any more"), and doesn't want to play with Jamey like he used to. When Jamey went in the house, his father was screaming at his mother, and had a gun pointed at her. She was duct taped to a chair, the tape across her mouth as well. It was not across her nose, and she was breathing. Jamey ran out of the house to a neighbor's and called the police.

What Joseph intends to do with his wife is unknown. Jamey is in hysterics, and at this time no more information can be gotten from the child. All he can say is, "My daddy is really being weird."

1 – Criminal History

Joseph has a minor arrest record: Minor in Possession x 2, one DUI at age 19, and an Assault 4 (pled down after he broke someone's jaw in a melee in a bar at the age of 22).

1 – Interview with Family Member

Negotiators must first locate and find a family member to interview. The director should have an idea of how this could occur. There are many ways a witness or family member could be located, and so the director needs to be open minded to ways that would work. However, <u>do not just give this information away—make your team work hard for it.</u> The Intel negotiator should explain to the director how they would go about looking for information: talking to the son, looking in his cell phone for numbers, talking to neighbors, finding work mates who might know more about the family, etc. You can have the Intel negotiator work a little to find the right person, have one lead reveal another, etc., until they actually make contact with the family member, or whoever has the information the team needs. The director of the exercise can determine whom the family member should be, given what role players you have available. If no actual person is playing the part, a suggestion might be to make the family member the wife's sister. The wife shared with her sister how she was sometimes frightened of her husband.

INFORMATION ACQUIRED FROM FAMILY MEMBERS

Joseph's immediate family (mother, father, brothers and sisters) has no history of any major mental illness. An uncle was said to be bipolar, but how the family knows that is unclear. Joseph used to party, but by all reports had settled down. He's been working as an independent contractor, mostly doing home remodels. He's been having problems at the job site the last couple of months, getting angry quickly, and others say that he sometimes makes inconsistent demands, and changes his mind a lot.

Information from collateral contacts

Essential information will only be revealed if the interviewer asks the right questions. The family member role player is free to adopt any kind of role (belligerent, scared, cautious), and the interviewer must effectively work with whatever they present. The family member, however, must give the information if the interviewer is effective. If the interviewer is 'phoning it in,' is rude or rushed, terminate the call or contact

---

1 – First Contact with Negotiator

Joseph, upon first contact, sounds buoyant and happy, but on the edge of being out of control. He says he had twenty-two hours and seventeen minutes of things to say to his wife, and she kept interrupting, so he taped her up so he could be sure she stayed still to listen. He tells the officer to wait because he's got to be in top shape and he drops the phone, does 25 push-ups, and picks up the phone again to continue talking. This happens repeatedly (the role player, if they can't do the exercises, should put the phone down and breathe as if they are doing them - - - - (or, if the coach from the negotiation team is in the room, they can do the exercise).

He is volatile, and will talk very rapidly. He will be easily irritated, misunderstands what the officer says, and goes off on a lot of tangents. He is also provocative, saying things to get a rise out of the officer. The best image for the role player is that talking to him should be like trying to hold mercury in your hand—every time you think you have a 'hold' on him, he will 'slip through your fingers.'

1 – Interview with a neighbor and Jamey, who has now calmed down

Jamey has been in the neighbor's care. The neighbor has been trying to get law enforcement's attention for quite some time, so he will present as frustrated. Jamey is worried because he doesn't have his pills (medication). He's worried for two reasons—he hasn't taken them today, and the bottle was almost empty, though he thought he had a lot more. Jamey was going to tell his mother, but he forgot. Jamey says he takes pills to help him concentrate in school, "because I can't sit still and do what I'm supposed to." He says the pills "are called Adival or Addital or Amital or something like that."

1 – Further Interviewing with Joseph, After Getting Info Regarding Son

Joseph, when asked, tells the officer the school told him his son has ADHD, which " . . . is a lie. He's just smart and bored. But my wife made him go to the doctor and take the meds. I love my son. I don't want him to take something that's bad for him. So I've been taking them too, both to see what effect they have and out of solidarity."

1 – Psych Consult Regarding Bipolar Subjects

If you haven't picked it up already, the consultant will suggest the strong possibility Joseph is manic, either because he has bipolar disorder, or due to his taking his son's medications, which are stimulants. You will recognize the manic person because they will display super high energy. They will often be talking very fast and their ideas will 'zigzag' from one to another. They often act like comedians, with a rapid-fire delivery. Their behavior may also be either sexualized or hair-trigger aggressive. In either case, they will very likely be provocative. Here are some things you should do:

- Remain calm and centered;
- Be conscious of their 'brittle' state of mind, in spite of how confidently they behave. Grandiose doesn't mean strong! So, if you question their competence, or make them feel vulnerable or silly, they may explode with rage;
- Don't bluntly criticize their actions;
- Don't laugh at them, either deliberately, or involuntarily;
- Don't join in what sounds like fun. It isn't;
- If you use any humor, it is for the purpose of slowing them down, not joking around. If you joke around, you will 'wind them up.' They may start to fool around like they are a character in a cartoon, where no one *really* gets hurt—they just 'see stars.' Or, they may be caught off-guard by your humor and they will think you are laughing at them;
- They may try to provoke you (think of the Road Runner and Coyote);
- They can be very volatile, exploding into rage with the slightest provocation. Be relaxed but ready for the worst.

If the manic person is also psychotic, the psychosis, particularly the delusions, will probably take precedence. In these situations, you essentially have a hallucinating or delusional person who also happens to be moving and talking very fast.

SCENARIO 1 – Checklist for After Action Review

The after action assessment/critique will depend on what was expressed and expected of the team going into the exercise. In other words, what was the desired training goal or outcome? Not just the outcome of the scenario, but what are the skills the director (team leader) is hoping to see exercised by the team, as these scenarios/situations develop?

Team established floor plan in timely manner?
- ❑ Did not meet goal
- ❑ Partially met goal
- ❑ Fully met goal

Team recognized what was going on with subject?
- ❑ Did not meet goal
- ❑ Partially met goal
- ❑ Fully met goal

Negotiator dealt appropriately with subject?
- ❑ Did not meet goal
- ❑ Partially met goal
- ❑ Fully met goal

Negotiator demonstrated good listening skills?
- ❑ Did not meet goal
- ❑ Partially met goal
- ❑ Fully met goal

Negotiator did not challenge or criticize subject?
- ❑ Did not meet goal
- ❑ Partially met goal
- ❑ Fully met goal

SCENARIO 2

Child Molestation, Coercion, Kidnap, Brittle Narcissism

2 – Background Information

Samuel Matheson is thirteen years old. His parents called police several weeks ago. When they went to his 2nd story room to wake him up for school, he was gone. They found a ladder underneath an open window. They searched his computer, and found a 28-year-old male, Henry Monroe, had befriended him on line, unbeknownst to Samuel's family. As best as can be determined, Henry travelled to Samuel's town, and got him to climb out the window into his waiting arms. The two of them left together. Based on appearances (a backpack gone, several pairs of clothes, toiletries, and a stuffed animal) Samuel went to him voluntarily. They have been on the run for two weeks.

This incident has been on America's Most Wanted or some other similar TV show.

2 – Call to the Parents

9-1-1 gets a call from the parents. Samuel called his parents on the phone a few minutes ago, sounding very confused: he talked about how Henry understood and loved him, but Samuel sounded scared and weary as well. He alluded to wanting to come home, even getting tearful, but then got defiant, saying his mom and dad never understood him. He hung up the phone, saying Henry would take care of him.

The parents are going to be very upset. The role player can either play the role as scared or somewhat hysterical, so it will be hard to get accurate information.

Working with 9-1-1 Call-takers

The 9-1-1 call-taker will be responsible for passing the information on to the negotiation team. The training goal is for the call-taker to get practice in getting through the noise and emotion, and conveying all the accurate information to the negotiation team.

---

2 – Subjects Located—Call from Motel Owner

A motel owner, recognizing the 'couple' from America's Most Wanted, tried to be heroic, and hammered on the door, yelling, "Come out of there, you fucking pervert, and leave that boy alone. I will kick your ass, you damn faggot." Henry yelled through the door that he would kill anyone who came in, and why couldn't they just be left alone in peace. The motel owner eventually called police. Officers respond, confirm the information, locate the suspect's room, and contain the occupants. Officers request SWAT and HNT.

The motel owner is going to be chest-puffing belligerent, really angry, cursing out pedophiles, homosexuals in general and accusing the police of dragging their feet due to the 'atheistic homo lobby' running the government these days

Nothing more is known about the current situation. It is not known if they have any weapons, if there has been sexual contact, why the two of them are together, or if Samuel is still fully or partially willing to be with Henry or is held against his will.

2 – Criminal Background Check

No history of violence in his adult record. There is some indication of a juvenile record. It will take time to get the juvenile record, which is sealed.

2 – Interview with Henry's Relatives

Because most of Henry's criminal history took place as a juvenile, unlikely it would come up in a criminal history check. This is an example of where the director has to do a little problem solving to figure out how the team is going to gather Intel on Henry. Since we know from the original call that there was information on him from the "America's Most Wanted", etc., info is available. Perhaps (and more than likely) Henry has a Facebook page. (**This can be set up in advance by the team coordinator).** If you have a computer savvy member on your team, and they check out Henry's Facebook, that could reveal leads to a lot of the Intel you wish for them to uncover…maybe his sister's name (or other relative); maybe he discusses his thoughts, desires, philosophies on Facebook.

Concerning social media

Do not confine your search to Facebook. There are a number of other social media sites more popular with many these days. Other popular sites include Twitter, LinkedIn, Pinterest, Google+, Tumblr, Instagram, VK, Flickr and Vine, to name a few. Even MySpace, considered to be out of fashion, is still used, particularly by many with 'alternative' lifestyles. A general project for your team should be to assemble data on all these conduits of information.

Contact with Cousin

Henry has some history in another state, according to a relative, of being a 'sexually aggressive youth'— but the records are sealed and more details have not yet been accessed. He was apparently quite young at the time of whatever happened.

He is a member of a pacifist group—adamantly anti-war and vegetarian.

2 – Contact with Henry's Brother

At age fifteen, Henry was involved in an incident at his church. According to records, he was a former youth group leader. He was accused of an 'unwholesome' interest in a twelve year old boy in the youth group. The boy in the youth group's mother stated her son started to get secretive. She read his diary and there were romantic poems about Henry. She caught him sneaking out of the house to meet Henry, and she called police. Henry denied any special contact or interest in the youth. He resigned from the church group. There were no charges.

Henry had a psychological assessment at age seventeen, at the demand of his parents. The brother has read the report. The psychologist said Henry did not, at that time, show any violent impulses, nor did he have violent fantasies. However, he was very immature, and found boys his own age to be intimidating. He had always played with kids younger than him, and his sexual interest was primarily with boys just approaching the teen years.

2 – For the Role Player

Henry is a pretentious guy. He intersperses his conversation with a lot of "you know what I mean" phrases, and alludes to travel to Europe, visits to fine museums, beautiful vistas. He sprinkles his sentences with phrases in French. It's unclear if he's ever been to Europe, or if he can speak French, knows ballet, etc.

This is an example. The role player should have several hobbies, travel experience or other interests that they can use to build the role. If they speak another language, they are free to use that.

Henry will have a prissy manner—but NOT someone's stereotype of a 'queen.' More like an arrogant prep school graduate. Henry will be disdainful and contemptuous:

- If the officer is male and attempts to be friendly or jocular, or if he softens his voice offering to help, Henry should be flirtatious, trying to push the officer's buttons.
- If the officer, male or female, is cold or matter-of-fact, Henry is going to act offended.
- Henry will try to impress the negotiator with his knowledge, hobbies, or whatever his pre-occupations are. He'll go off on tangents, and it will be very hard to get him back on track.

When the officer tries to ascertain Samuel's well-being, Henry will get outraged anyone would imagine he might intend to hurt Samuel. You may hear Samuel weeping or crying in the background.

On Scenarios Involving children characters

This role-play—and many others—will be too raw for a real kid, so either a high voiced adult or a tape of someone crying and asking to leave should be played in the background. If it's going to be verbally heard and not visually observed, often a female voice works well for an adolescent male. If you have exceptionally 'young acting' students at a college level, they can be suitable.

Henry will try to reassure Samuel. HOWEVER, as the negotiation goes on, and Samuel continues to be upset, Henry will get increasingly irritable, offended with Samuel that he is distressed.

As Henry gets anxious, he is going to start accusing the officers as leaving him no way out, that the cops are all homophobic. He will start to push some buttons, talking about how loving men should initiate youth in manhood, and no one loves the beauty of the young spirit like a man such as he. He will state sex is a vehicle to the spirit of youth.

2 – Psychological Consultation

Henry's pretentiousness and speechifying is a manifestation of narcissism. He is not only in love with himself; he is the only important thing in the universe. His molesting of youth is an expression of entitlement. He is dangerous to Samuel, because in his view, Samuel cannot help but love him. He extinguishes the reality of who Samuel is, to maintain his fantasy of this pure love of older man to youth. As the negotiation drags on and Samuel gets more frightened and upset, Henry will very likely get increasingly outraged Samuel is not on the 'same page.'

The negotiator should try to begin to establish rapport by subtle admiration for his sophistication and wide knowledge. In other words, the negotiator tries to successfully link Henry to all the things he thinks are special in his life and in himself. The reason is this: you want Henry to think he is too special to die. You cannot say this, but he will assume this himself if he is 'allowed' to go on about his specialness. Because he feels he has an audience, he will likely begin to 'believe his own press' about how wonderful he is. The officer must be able to tolerate this—including his specialness as a lover of boys.

The goal is this: Henry must still feel like he has a lot to lose. It can be framed, at the proper moment, that he really hasn't committed much of a crime. He hasn't 'kidnapped' the child—Samuel went voluntarily.

Warning! Tripwires with Narcissistic Individuals

If the officer happens to know a lot about what Henry claims to be interested in, s/he must be careful! Henry may not know much about the subject after all, and when the officer displays his/her knowledge, Henry will be embarrassed at being found out, resulting in a breaking of rapport, even rage. He needs to feel himself to be special, and if the officer is smarter than he is, he's lost his specialness.

What will make Henry most dangerous is if his sense of specialness is questioned or challenged. If he doesn't have himself, he has nothing. This most certainly encompasses his self-image.

SCENARIO 2 – Checklist for After Action Review

The after action assessment/critique will depend on what was expressed and expected of the team going into the exercise. In other words, what was the desired training goal or outcome? Not just the outcome of the scenario, but what are the skills the director (team leader) is hoping to see exercised by the team, as these scenarios/situations develop?

Floor plan established in a timely manner?
- ❏ Did not meet goal
- ❏ Partially met goal
- ❏ Fully met goal

Team proceeded with ideas for Intel gathering/suggestions
- ❏ Did not meet goal
- ❏ Partially met goal
- ❏ Fully met goal

Primary negotiator was able to check his/her own attitude toward subject
- ❏ Did not meet goal
- ❏ Partially met goal
- ❏ Fully met goal

Negotiator demonstrated good listening skills
- ❏ Did not meet goal
- ❏ Partially met goal
- ❏ Fully met goal

Negotiator demonstrated a non-judgmental attitude
- ❏ Did not meet goal
- ❏ Partially met goal
- ❏ Fully met goal

SCENARIO 3

Overtly Sociopathic Teen

3 – Original Call

A 12-year-old girl at a 7-11 store reports that her family is being threatened and held at knifepoint by her sister's boyfriend at a nearby location.

Officers respond, determine the residence, contain, and request SWAT and HNT.

3 – Interviews with Store Owner and Child

> **On Scenarios Involving Children's Characters**
> This role-play—and many others—will be too raw for a real kid, so either a high voiced adult or a tape of someone crying and asking to leave should be played in the background. If it's going to be verbally heard and not visually observed, often a female voice works well for an adolescent male. If you have exceptionally 'young acting' students at a college level, they can be suitable.

The storeowner is going to have the bare bones facts only. The 'child' role player should be coached by your child interview specialist, a therapist or child protective services social worker familiar with children in crises/violent situations. You will either interview her yourself, or have another member of that team do the interview. A good interview should acquire all the necessary information such as the home layout, the situation, etc. The role player should, realistically, make this difficult, so the interviewer gets a good chance to practice interviewing a child.

Another excellent option, get a child-interview detective involved, and have them 'present' to the HNT members the facts of the case, as if they had done the interview with the child already. They should have worked with the director, and developed the facts of this case, and asked the questions that they would ask. This is a time saving option, as well as a good alternative if you do not have someone who can convincingly play a 12 year old that has been traumatized.

In either event, a proper interview with the child will reveal:

Jesse, age seventeen, was visiting his girlfriend, and was engaged in sex with her when her folks came home with their other daughter, aged twelve. Her father blew up in rage at seeing his daughter, age 14, despoiled on the couch, but Jesse grabbed his folder-knife and cut the man on the cheek. Jesse was so intimidating that he held mother, father and girlfriend 'motionless' with his will while he put on his clothes—but not before engaging in about ten minutes more sex with his girlfriend in front of the family.

He began ordering the family members to fetch him things, and otherwise dominated them. He has not allowed the daughter to dress. Finally, as if to test his dominance, he told the twelve year old to go to the 7-11 down the street and get him a coke, saying he'd kill the family if she didn't return. She burst out crying at the 7-11, the clerk got the story out of her, and called police.

The father is a gun collector, but the daughter doesn't know if Jesse knows this, or has the key to the cabinet. The interviewer will only get this information, if he or she thinks to ask. If not, Jesse is going to be armed with a gun, as well as knives, and the police will not know it.

3 – Interview with Friends

Managing Information with multiple interviewees, particularly adolescents

A good practice interview would be with two or three friends, who all chime in together, some with extraneous details, and others with relevant facts. This will be good practice in information management.

Remember, the director needs to come up with some ideas for how the team is going to confirm Jesse's ID, and find friends to interview. Maybe the 12 yr old sister knows his last name. She probably knows the school her sister (and <possibly> Jesse) attends. The director should have some ideas in mind, but the team is apt to come up with ideas not yet considered.

Jesse Holliday is seventeen. He has a several year history of substance abuse. He likes mushrooms because he's always had interesting visions, but his favorite substance is crystal meth. He also smokes weed and drinks.

He's got several accusations of date rape, but no charges were ever pressed. He was kicked off the basketball team when the coach told him he was 'dogging it.' Jesse threw the ball at point blank range in the coach's face, breaking his nose.

3 – Interview with Jesse's Parents

Their tone should be concerned, clueless and dismayed

His parents are on scene and they seem to be ordinary folks. They've got two other kids, no trouble whatsoever, but Jesse has always been different. They are at a total loss to explain why. They twice had him in counseling: Jesse made one counselor cry three sessions in a row, at which point the counselor quit; the other ended up writing him a love-letter that Jesse got his mother to mail to the licensing board. Jesse claimed he was traumatized and has been working with a lawyer to file a damage suit.

His parents put him in martial arts, hoping the discipline would help. In particular, Jesse has trained two years in Filipino Kali, which specializes in the use of the dagger. He loves knives—he throws them, he carries them, and one of his favorite tricks has been to whip out his blade and slash it at top speed at a friend's throat, turning it over at the last second so that the flat of the blade goes across the carotid. He's scratched one or two people, and terrified many. (His parents wonder if maybe it wasn't a good idea that they let him study this).

3 – The Scene
The windows are blocked with blankets. Jesse's been moving the family through the big several story house; you don't know what room they are in.

3 – Negotiations
Jesse will be very provocative. He will be obscene and vicious. He will register to anything and everything you say, listening for weak points and for leverage, to knock you off balance, or ideally, to anger you. For example, he will only talk to you if you accept him calling you "Officer Fuck." (The negotiator will be stuck in the fine dilemma of not being defiant and offended, but also not being a pushover).

Jesse will not be making concrete demands for the most part, although he may demand something off the wall, like a scallop burrito, or the like. If you bring him something he does demand, he may throw it back out a window.

Coordination with SWAT #1

This is an excellent scenario to practice either as an extended, high-adrenalin negotiation, or for the integration of SWAT to enter the home and neutralize the threat.

Escalation, which would result in SWAT intervention, can be built into the scenario with alternatives such as:

1. Jesse has the daughter half-shoved out an upper story window, holding his knife close to her neck
2. Jesse forces one family member to jump out of an upper story window
3. He gets into a shouting match with the father, cuts him and you hear screaming and pleas to "Stop! Stop!"

---

3 – Psychological/Tactical Consult

The negotiator could use the usual tactic of suggesting to Jesse that although this could develop into a bad situation, it isn't yet. He was engaged in sex, yes, and when startled, reacted perhaps too aggressively, but if he lets people go now, this is something that can be worked out. He's still a minor, he's a smart, articulate guy, and he should be able to explain his situation to people. If the negotiator is successful in getting Jesse to think of what he believes is his long-term interest, he could let the hostages go and surrender. With a character like Jesse, this appeal to his grandiosity and self-regard is always a 'first gambit'—and in cases where the sociopathic subject wants to survive, this often works.

Coordination with SWAT #2 (The tactic of negotiation is sound, but SWAT is still needed)

Activation of SWAT even with success: Even if the exercise is set up 'successfully,' SWAT, in reality or simulation, should be fully activated. For example, Jesse could surrender and then, at the last minute, change his mind, grab his 'girlfriend' and try to get back into the house.

Activation of SWAT with entry into home: The writers believe this exercise is ideal to be programmed for SWAT entry into the home. In this case, do NOT program in a *successful* appeal to his narcissism, where he agrees he's too special to suffer consequences (whether or not he has a last second change of plans). Instead, he will perceive you as trying to play him and he will escalate to the point that SWAT must act.

Given this seems to be a 'victim taking' rather than a 'hostage taking,' the negotiator's task is to keep Jesse on the line as long as possible, (so that SWAT can fully exercise their skills in this training exercise, just as they would in real life) Jesse can be considered an 'aggressive narcissist,' which is what a sociopath[4] truly is. As far as he is concerned, the only thing that matters is himself. Get him talking about himself. Do not give him obvious praise, but listen in a way that makes him think he has a 'captive audience,' who is impressed with him.

What will be most dangerous is if he perceives you as:
- Insulting him
- Questioning his seriousness
- Challenging him

He very likely will take this out on one of the hostages. He is essentially a sexual sadist—and is very likely to use his knife to mutilate or even kill one or all of the hostages.

To emphasize again, this should be regarded as a 'victim taking' scenario, not a 'hostage taking' situation, as there is really nothing to gain in what he is doing.

---

4   Although there are sometimes fine-grained debates in the psychological arena, the words psychopath and sociopath should be considered synonymous.

SCENARIO 3 – Checklist for After Action Review

The after action assessment/critique will depend on what was expressed and expected of the team going into the exercise. In other words, what was the desired training goal or outcome? Not just the outcome of the scenario, but what are the skills the director (team leader) is hoping to see exercised by the team, as these scenarios/situations develop?

Establish a floor plan in timely manner?
- ❏ Did not meet goal
- ❏ Partially met goal
- ❏ Fully met goal

Request a child interview detective?
- ❏ Did not meet goal
- ❏ Partially met goal
- ❏ Fully met goal

Ask about guns
- ❏ Did not meet goal
- ❏ Partially met goal
- ❏ Fully met goal

Did negotiators separate the friends before doing interviews?
- ❏ Did not meet goal
- ❏ Partially met goal
- ❏ Fully met goal

Did the primary negotiator remain unemotional from the personal attacks from subject?
- ❏ Did not meet goal
- ❏ Partially met goal
- ❏ Fully met goal

Was the team honest in their assessment/review of status of situation with command post regarding likely outcome
- ❏ Did not meet goal
- ❏ Partially met goal
- ❏ Fully met goal

SCENARIO 4

Control Freak, Paranoid Character

4 – Original Call

Report of shots fired at the Child Protective Services office. Caller states a man with a shotgun entered and fired into the ceiling, and kicked an employee in the face. He was observed entering a room with his children, an older female and a CPS employee. The last appears to be injured.

Officers responded, contained the building, then requested SWAT and HNT.

4 – Interview with Original Caller, A Social Worker, Who Meets the First Responder

A role player, very amped up will have the information here. They will report to one officer, who is responsible for passing the information on to the rest of the team

Roger McClafferty walked into the Child Protective Services (CPS) office blasting a shotgun into the ceiling. He hauled himself over the front desk, and when the receptionist tried to stop him, he kicked her in the face, knocking out several teeth. Followed by a social worker who ran towards, rather than away from the noise, McClafferty ran back to one of the visitation rooms where he found his two daughters, aged 4 and 7, visiting with their grandmother. Using the butt of the shotgun, he smashed the visit supervisor in the head. The observing social worker, at this point, ran out and assisted in clearing the building.

McClafferty was last seen in the visitation room with his two children, the grandmother (maternal side) and the unconscious social worker. The building has been cleared.

It is unknown where in the building McClafferty currently is, and what he has done with any of the hostages.

4 – Layout of Incident

Each visitation room has a viewing window from the inside of the hallway, but not the outside. They are on a narrow hallway, which two people can pass closely. The hallway has fire doors on each side, so if one doesn't pass by the head-high window, they will not be seen. However, the center of the office is a maze of cubicles. Each cube has a phone and a desk, and each has a screen approximately 6 feet, 8 inches in height. Some areas can be seen from the outside, if you are on a third floor looking in—although because the glass is reflective to keep out heat, one can see only shadows if the light is just right.

The building is modern, with high-tempered glass windows. The office is on the third floor—you will not be able to break in a window to throw in a phone. Equally, there is a clear field of fire and wide-open space, albeit cluttered with chairs in the lobby. To throw the phone over the front desk would expose any officer to potentially lethal fire.

McClafferty can call out from any phone. Social workers will know their own phone numbers, and somewhere there is a master list. It does not map the cubicles on the list, however.

McClafferty has the children, he has a shotgun, and he has a rather frail elderly woman as hostage and a probably unconscious woman as well. You don't know where he is.

A Detailed Layout

The information in the layout above can either be provided to the team, or can also be the product of an interview with another role player familiar with the building. It can also serve as an example of the kind of scene you want to set up to make an exercise that SWAT can also productively participate.

The detailed description of the layout is a two-fold suggestion:

1. If this will be a negotiator-only practice, it is a suitable 'as-if' situation.
2. On the other hand, this exercise is a good one for both SWAT and HNT, and can be set up to meet the tactical training needs SWAT may have. This might be an exercise where the SWAT trainer, working with the director, has the priority choice when selecting the venue for this exercise. If SWAT will also be incorporated in the exercise, it is a paradigm of a set-up where the environment is exceptionally difficult to an immediate entry, putting both officers and hostages at risk. The goal for the SWAT team leader would be to set up an environment to truly challenge the team's skills. Thus, it could shift into an active shooter situation, with HNT trying to fix the location of the hostage taker, and keep him occupied on the phone.

---

4 – Directions for Role Player

You should be argumentative and provocative. You will quibble about little things. "You said you'd call me in five minutes. It's been six!" Your speech should be over-controlled—say, "do not," rather than "don't." Speak as if you are biting your words. You are all about control—if you feel like the negotiator is controlling you, escalate. On the other hand, if the negotiator is too friendly or supportive, you will see this as trying to soften you up.

4 – Some possible demands you can fixate on

- You want to talk to your ex-wife to explain/convince her there was no sexual abuse—because "she's wrong in believing that."

- You want any allegations of sexual abuse removed from police reports
- You want allegations of DV removed from your criminal history—they weren't really your fault, after all
- You want more time (custody) with your children—you think your wife has brainwashed them

4 – Criminal Background Check

Since this will be a complex incident, it is suggested the first interview/information be obtained from the primary witness, the worker who observed the initial assaults. Wishing to make things move a bit faster in the beginning, the director can choose to allow that witness to know who this man is on site, and be able to identify him by name, and have some familiarity with his case. The director can choose (or not) to have this witness be the same caseworker who actually has this man's case, and therefore all the information relevant to this situation.

He has 7 arrests for domestic violence in his current marriage – and 5 from previous relationships. His wife recanted on the first six allegations. She left him on this, the seventh.

4 – Call to Ex-Wife

She will be bitter and want to talk about what a jerk he is. Furthermore, she will be angry the children were removed from her care as well, and she will focus on her own complaints with CPS. It will be hard to get her on task. She can reveal McClafferty has a history of recreational drug and alcohol use, but she does not know exactly what, or if he has used today.

4 – Interview with Social Worker Who Investigated the Case

For training purposes, the social worker should be extremely emotionally agitated. The interviewer will have to calm him or her down before getting solid information. Use either paraphrasing, or the calm, authoritative tone of someone in absolute competent control, to stabilize the interviewee enough to get the information.

McClafferty and his wife are estranged. Although of average intelligence, he prefers relationships with developmentally disabled women. They are easy to control, and unlikely to complain. Of his current wife, McClafferty has said, "I love her for her innocence. God help her, she's dumb as a post, but she knows enough to do what she's told."

Previous to this last allegation, the children were taken away due to severe neglect. They were going to school unwashed, wearing the same clothes for weeks at a time. Other children viciously teased them for their smell. The kids came to school several times with unexplained bruises—but no allegations of physical abuse were ever founded.

After the last allegation of physical abuse, his wife alleged he had been sexually abusing their daughters. She said she knew about it for a long time, but was 'too afraid' to do anything about it. When the girls were interviewed by a so-called "interview specialist," they described, circumstantially, sexual contact with both parents. According to the social worker, the interview was incredibly flawed, however, and there is legitimate debate that the children may have picked up on what the interviewer expected to hear. McClafferty has denied the allegations, and gets in a white-heat rage when he talks about it, saying once you are accused, there is no way out, and that Child Protective Services gets a commission on every kid in foster care.

Because of these allegations, neither parent has visitation rights. The maternal grandmother sees the children once a week. She is too elderly to care for the kids, and they have been in a foster home.

4 – Psychological Consultation

The paranoid individual has an attitude that it is always another person's fault if anything is wrong. Whether delusional or not, they see others as conspiring against them or persecuting them.

One helpful image of the paranoid person is an angry porcupine, all quills, with a soft underbelly, hunched over, ready to strike in hair-trigger reaction.

The paranoid individual (whether delusional or not) has a consistent *attitude* of blame, resentment of authority, fear of vulnerability, and an expectation of being betrayed by people they trust.

- Without compromising on any tactical issues, let them know what's going on, so there is no ambiguity. Because paranoid people are so suspicious, they will often quiz you concerning why you're doing something. Whenever you can, tell them what you're doing. At the same time, you shouldn't accept being quizzed incessantly. You aren't required to explain every action. In fact, it might be a tactic to throw you off guard or distract you.
- Be aware of both physical and emotional spacing. Maintain a correct distancing, neither too close nor too far. Keep your tone matter-of-fact. Speak in formal tones. Don't be too friendly. Try to be aware when things are getting too relaxed. If the paranoid person relaxes, they may suddenly startle, realizing that for a brief moment, they let their guard down. They may respond by exploding to make sure you don't "take them over."
- Watch your triggers; they will try to provoke you so they can "hit you back first." If you lose your temper, they will feel justified in whatever they do to you as well as it keying into their terror-based aggression. A slang expression for this is "fear biters." They bark and snarl and when you react, they attack as if you went after them first.
- Being mistaken or wrong is another form of vulnerability. They will try to engage you in an argument. If they are losing, they will escalate.
- Paranoid people examine your communication like detectives. They continually search for evidence to prove what they already know is true.
- Maintain your calm. The paranoid individual is usually assaultive when they feel under attack, when they perceive you as controlling them, or when they perceive that you are afraid.

- Be careful about 'active listening.' You can definitely paraphrase, but he may use your paraphrasing as support for his extreme positions. Also, if you sound too much like a 'psych' person, he will feel manipulated. Therefore, paraphrase in a matter-of-fact, ordinary way, like, "This is a bad situation." NOT "I hear you saying that you find yourself in a difficult place."
- The truth and his fiction are different. The truth, of course, is that he has hostages, and one, at least, is injured. You need to find out his demands. If you focus too much on the hostages, given he is a man of grievances, you will make them targets. His fiction is that the main problem is being accused of sexual abuse (it may actually be a false allegation, but his 'fiction' is this is the main problem at present). Therefore, the negotiator should focus on helping him find a way out of <u>that</u> situation, and releasing the hostages should be framed as a means to that end.

SCENARIO 4 – Checklist for After Action Review

The after action assessment/critique will depend on what was expressed and expected of the team going into the exercise. In other words, what was the desired training goal or outcome? Not just the outcome of the scenario, but what are the skills the director (team leader) is hoping to see exercised by the team, as these scenarios/situations develop?

Floor plan established
- ❏ Did not meet goal
- ❏ Partially met goal
- ❏ Fully met goal

Team satisfactorily deals with the demands to speak to ex
- ❏ Did not meet goal
- ❏ Partially met goal
- ❏ Fully met goal

Demonstrates good listening skills
- ❏ Did not meet goal
- ❏ Partially met goal
- ❏ Fully met goal

Does Intel determine the right people necessary to interview and find them?
- ❏ Did not meet goal
- ❏ Partially met goal
- ❏ Fully met goal

Does team recognize they are dealing with a fearful, paranoid person? Staying calm is the key
- ❏ Did not meet goal
- ❏ Partially met goal
- ❏ Fully met goal

SCENARIO 5

Depression, Survivor Guilt

5 – Original Call

Neighbors called police to report shots fired, and the sound of glass breaking at the house next door to (location). There is a broken window in the front of the house. Officers respond, and set up containment. Either request communications call inside, or responding officers make the call with a cell phone. The subject is contacted. He says, "Go away. I just want to die," then hangs up the phone. Officers request SWAT and HNT.

Officers place a second call in and the person answering has the same response as before. "Go away. I just want to die." He is not, however, responsive to the question whether someone else is in the house. At this point, you have several alternatives:

- Continue over the phone (safest), making it into a 'table-top' exercise;
- Continue with either a throw phone or other technology, on scene, having the officers call for additional units, and then approach the house, and try to make contact. (Delivery of throw phone is a good exercise for SWAT).

When the officers attempt to engage the homeowner, they hear tearful screams, followed by quiet pleading to just "leave me alone. I don't want to hurt you guys – just leave me in peace so I can maybe get up the guts this time to die right. Then again, maybe you should stay around. I'm probably such a coward that I'll fuck this up as well. Maybe you can do it for me." (This last sentence should definitely get the attention of the officers).

Investigation quickly reveals this is the home of Joseph Creighton, where a horrendous crime took place a number of months ago.

5 – Call from Friend/Relative

As always, all of this information is available, but unless the interviewer does an effective interview, they will not get it. This role player should be vague and a little worried. They will dither around—it will be hard to get them to say something directly. They will allude to Joseph having general problems with depression because "something bad happened." If the interviewer gets impatient, the role player will get offended and hang up the phone, saying, "I was just trying to help and this is the thanks I get."

If the negotiators are resourceful, they will check with neighbors, or, once they identify the subject by name, and run the name, they will uncover the crime that had taken place. They should be able to access all kinds of info…the police investigation, in addition to newspaper accounts, since this was a high profile case. Also, neighbors would likely have additional information regarding the mental state, etc. of Joseph. This is a scenario where the director can have all kinds of information prepared to 'reward' the negotiations team for doing good, thorough Intel work.

Once this information is gathered, you should be able to utilize your department "in house" records to confirm what the friend/relative has told you.

Joseph Creighton was the father of three kids, and a beautiful wife. They had the relationship anyone would dream of, and this was not just an illusion. He had a job he loved, as a specialist in protecting endangered species, and his wife, Charlotte, was a dynamic prosecutor specializing in felony prosecutions. Their children, 14-year-old Brittany, 12-year-old Clayton, and 9-year-old Erica were bright, athletic and charming.

One and one-half years ago, Chris Monckton, invaded the home. Monckton had been prosecuted 7 years earlier by Charlotte Spencer-Creighton, and due to her aggressive and thorough work, Monckton was not allowed to plea bargain on an assault II charge (he had a nasty history) and he was given more than the standard sentencing range. He served his time, and was released.

He killed the children and Charlotte with a knife. Joseph survived because when Monckton kicked his way into the house, Joseph ran through the house and out the back. He did yell to his family to run, but the girls were upstairs, and Charlotte was first killed, trying to fight Monckton and protect their daughters rather than flee.

Safe outside, Joseph heard the murders, and his shouts for help brought neighbors and law enforcement – too late.

Monckton gave up without a struggle—with a smirk actually—and is held in jail. His lawyer has successfully gotten repeated continuances, and the case is in limbo.

Joseph has been increasingly depressed for months, has cut himself off from his family and friends.

He has abandoned his hygiene. You will hear from friends and family that he has been talking to himself—he is quite distracted, and he may be hearing voices.

5 – Psychological Consultation

This man is severely depressed, and he has good reason to be so. Severe depression is a state of extreme isolation. The subject usually feels cut off from humanity. To make things worse in this case, Mr. Creighton truly is cut-off. All of his loved ones were murdered, and he ran away, while his wife fought.

Do not try to comfort him by telling him that he did the best he could, and no one would think he is a coward. Do not assure him he couldn't have helped anyway. Do not try to offer him hope, that his work on behalf of endangered species is needed, and he, therefore, has a good reason to life. If you consider your own values, you may find yourself thinking were you this man, you would kill yourself as well. You will wonder how someone could live with himself, knowing he was a coward when he was most needed.

5 – Style of Communication

<u>Act as if you have all the time in the world.</u> We do not mean you act casually—simply that you don't rush anything. If you act like there is little time, the person you're talking with will believe you, and they'll rush to a decision or conclusion. <u>When you take time, you give time.</u> The suicidal person begins to believe there is enough time to figure out a better solution than suicide.

An overly gentle, 'concerned' voice will shut him down. He may be crying, but do not speak to him like he is a child. He feels weak and is disgusted with his weakness. If your voice is too soft, he will agree with you and become more and more dangerous. He may believe himself too weak to kill himself and will initiate a forced-police shooting (aka 'suicide-by-cop').

Do not, however, put too much confidence in your voice. If you present yourself as too 'together,' he will experience this as a slap in the face. Your voice would then implicitly suggest that you are the kind of man or woman who would NOT run away and leave his wife and children to be cut up with a knife. Speak easily, but with seriousness and gravity. A calm, matter-of-fact tone shows that you aren't panicked by their situation and that you can handle anything they say.

Use your voice to change his brain. Right now, his brain confirms his alienation and isolation. He is alone in the world. You are talking to prove to him he is not alone, the evidence is the dialogue, not that you say so. A respectful conversation conveys on an almost primal level that the suicidal person is still worth something because you find them worthwhile.

5 – Suicide Assessment

You need to ask if he intends to kill himself. Directly. Don't tiptoe around the subject, as vague statements leave the person an 'out.'

The four basic questions to assess suicide are:
- "Are you planning to kill yourself?"
- "How would you do it?"

- "Do you have the means to do it?"
- "When will you do it?"

If he's willing to talk about his suicidal thoughts, you can flesh things out with some of the following.

As you pace him and paraphrase, a question comes up: What has stopped you before today? Be sure not to make him feel like he 'failed' when he wasn't successful in a previous suicide attempt. In other words, "Why did you choose life before?" When they recall someone or something that stopped them, this may help them regain a sense of responsibility for the people who care for them, or some other factor that kept them alive in the past.

Try to assess if he's been using drugs or drinking. First of all, this is a significant risk factor that often decreases as they become more sober. Beyond this, sometimes this can be a leverage point, where you suggest that killing oneself is not a decision one should make while intoxicated. (The problem, however, is that they may be too intoxicated to see the logic of this).

Try to find out why he decided to be suicidal today. Again, this may not help 'solve' his problem, but it keeps him talking.

Be very careful about giving him advice. Given this situation, can you honestly think of anything that will make things better? Simple communication brings people away from suicide, even without a solution to the problems driving a person towards it.

Don't make any guarantees how much better life might be. Don't forget for a second that he let his wife and kids get slaughtered and did nothing. There is no better you can offer.

Remember, with this man, dialogue is the lifeline. He may actually surrender if you establish a strong enough connection that he feels responsible for taking up your time, or "I wouldn't want to do that to you." On the other hand, he may simply kill himself to stop inconveniencing you.[5]

Suicide by Cop Scenario
Although the basic scenario is set up as a potential suicide, the director could set it up as a 'suicide by cop,' with only minimal changes, in which officers may have to witness/be involved in the death of someone with whom they have developed a bond).

---

[5]   Because this is such an obvious point, one that we are sure officers have already learned, we have placed it in a footnote rather than the text. Nonetheless, we would be remiss if we didn't cover all bases. To whit: Do not dare the suicidal person to 'do it,' similar to saying to the chronic 'cutter,' "if you were serious, you'd cut lengthwise." It would be particularly stupid in this case, because he already knows himself to be a coward. Your dare could lead him either to kill himself or go outside to confront the officers. Officers are most likely to be tempted to do this if the subject whines, feels sorry for himself, lacks dignity or otherwise communicates in a way that you find repulsive.

5 – Training Note

This training exercise could very productively be set up that after a long negotiation, Joseph kills himself. You can, thereby, include a debriefing/after-action review of such a suicide after a long negotiation <u>as part of the training exercise.</u> Consider your debriefing procedures, peer support, etc. If this exercise is done effectively, you may bring up some real emotions, though it is merely a role play, and it can actually help train your peer support/after-action procedures to prepare for the inevitable times when such an incident does occur.

This is a really good exercise for beginning negotiators. Many new negotiators struggle with the concept of asking someone if they want to die, or if they are feeling "suicidal". Most people (including trained police officers) are a bit squeamish about asking outright. Officers, and especially hostage negotiators, have to be comfortable talking about suicide and discussing it in a matter of fact, and non-judgmental manner. The more practice, the better the skills.

SCENARIO 5 – Checklist for After Action Review

The after action assessment/critique will depend on what was expressed and expected of the team going into the exercise. In other words, what was the desired training goal or outcome? Not just the outcome of the scenario, but what are the skills the director (team leader) is hoping to see exercised by the team, as these scenarios/situations develop?

Establish floor plan
- ❏ Did not meet goal
- ❏ Partially met goal
- ❏ Fully met goal

Demonstrate good listening skills
- ❏ Did not meet goal
- ❏ Partially met goal
- ❏ Fully met goal

Good thorough Intel
- ❏ Did not meet goal
- ❏ Partially met goal
- ❏ Fully met goal

Primary negotiator willing to confront the suicidal ideation head on?
- ❏ Did not meet goal
- ❏ Partially met goal
- ❏ Fully met goal

Does team recognize the possibility of suicide by cop?
- ❏ Did not meet goal
- ❏ Partially met goal
- ❏ Fully met goal

Demonstrate extreme patience
- ❏ Did not meet goal
- ❏ Partially met goal
- ❏ Fully met goal

SCENARIO 6

Paranoid Character, Honor Obsessive

6 – Original Call

Contact is made with a woman regarding custodial interference. Complainant states she has full custody of her children, but her husband has taken their daughters from school. She says he has them at his home. She will meet officers a block away from (location)

Officers respond, and complainant takes them to subject's location. When contacted, subject refuses to open the door.

Victor Mroz took his daughters from school, and drove home with them. His wife has full custody, and he has only scheduled, supervised visits. His wife called the police.

6 – Initial Contact

Police contact him by phone. He will not open the door. He will say he does not mean to harm them; rather, it's about time someone cooked them some good food, and he bought them some new dresses. Officers will advise him he is guilty of custodial interference, and he needs to release the children and come out. Mroz states he would not. He tells officers he was in the military, and he knows how to fight. He does not wish to hurt police officers, but is armed and ready to fight and die to keep his children.

He states he served his country faithfully, but his country has broken faith with him. Therefore, he is declaring independence from the United States, and anyone who trespasses on his property will be considered a hostile invader. He says, "You should know with whom you are dealing," and gives his DD form 214 number. Officers hear the sound of a firearm being ratcheted, and Mroz terminates the call. HNT and SWAT are called.

6 – Contact from Officer in DV Unit

Bringing other units in to your training exercise

If your department has a DV unit, engage a DV detective to participate in this exercise, as if they had this prior case, and they were providing this background info for HNT.

Victor has been stalking his wife for six months. She got a restraining order when he wouldn't stop calling her. After the order was in place, the phone calls stopped.

She got custody of the children: three daughters aged 6, 8, and 9. He has told the DV detective over the phone, in cold, measured tones, he believes she is a slob, sending them to school without dressing them up to look pretty, and with lousy food—salami sandwiches, for example—for lunch.

According to the wife, some strange things subsequently happened that she believed were done by Victor, although she could not prove it. Per the DV detective's report, the mother called about a month ago, claiming she was run off the road by a car that looks like his. There was a fire set at her home four months ago, with an accelerant. This was expertly done: it looked like a prank, a trash fire, but the trash bin had been moved so it would ignite some paint cans, which had also been moved. If the mother had not stepped outside to smoke a cigarette, the house would have burned up. The girls were on overnights with friends on both cases, rather than with their mother.

Victor stated to the detective that he loves his children. He has denied any responsibility for the two incidents, accusing his wife of setting the fire and faking being driven off the road. As for his frequent calls—what others have called harassment—he says that it was done for honorable reasons: to convince his wife she should give the girls to him to raise, because he would treasure them like three princesses. The courts did not agree nor does his wife.

The DV detective states it is her understanding that Victor has considerable experience in the military, in special operations units.

6 – Contact with Military

It would be excellent practice for the HNT to try to utilize, and become familiar with various vet/military resources that would enable them to find a contact for cases like this. Resources that can help police are out there, but it takes some effort to find them. Sadly, it is going to be increasingly likely that an HNT might need a resource like that. Rather than inventing such an informant, who hands the team this information, we would like to see the team work harder for it, and advance their own resource list as a result. They can make calls as a hypothetical, giving the information they have, and see where they are next directed. At a certain point, if they have successfully followed the links, they will receive the following information: A former military guy who has a hobby of listening in on police scanners puts a call out to some buddies and a call comes in from a man who served in Somalia and other hot spots in the Middle East.

He states Victor is a scary guy. He is from Albania, but also Roma (commonly known as gypsies), who were badly treated in every country in Europe. He came to America as a teenager, and left the Roma community, wanting to be an American. He joined the military and served three tours in spec ops. He has medals up to his eyebrows.

"He was a strange guy. We called him Spooky. Nah, nothing to do with spies, or anything like that. But the man was quiet all the time. He was quiet when he was fighting, be it street warfare, with the bullets flying all around, or in some bar fight. Always had a little smile on his lips. But every once in a while he'd get mad, It was always over him thinking someone insulted him, and the man had no brake pedal, you know what I mean. He just wouldn't stop. He'd brood about it, he'd talk about it, but if he decided to go, the individual he was mad at better be in another country! I went with him to get tattoos. I got the usual shit: Semper Fi on one shoulder, a little devil on the other. He got 'Never forgive, never forget.' He had it put over his frickin' heart.'"

6 – Information from a Friend of the Family

The wife gives HNT this contact, who when interviewed, informs HNT: Victor is fifty-three, and in great shape. He just retired from working as an investigator, working to find mitigating circumstances in death penalty cases. Many people think this is a paradox, given his history and what they see as his values.

"Victor's a man who lives by a code he made for himself. His clan, I guess that's the way to say it, were real Roma. They lived in caravans, a really aimless lifestyle. Some of them, he's said, were real criminals. He joined the military, and it became his new culture. He went into the Special Forces. He's used to acting alone; that's why he liked being an investigator. He loves lost causes. He's also got a temper like you wouldn't believe. He's real cool about almost anything, but it's like a switch gets tripped, and once that happens, man, you just clear out. I was with him once when that happened at a neighborhood picnic. He thought someone said something rude: swore, or something, in front of his daughters, and he just started to burn. He told everyone to clear the area, because he could not answer for what he'd do if we didn't all leave right now. Next day he apologized, went house to house and gave each family a pretty expensive present. He said his daughters were his treasures, and he just couldn't accept what America was becoming, and how that might hurt his girls. And when he heard Al swear, he just had to make it stop right away. What was weird was he didn't say he 'lost it.' He was real cold. He just said, 'I had to make it stop.'"

6 – For the Role Player

Victor states he is declaring independence from the United States and all its laws. He is making his home an independent country. He is owed, he says, for his service to the United States, "my former country." His demands are simple. Once a month, he will release funds from his bank account for groceries to a former member of his military unit. He will also email him a shopping list, and he will buy food and clothes. Victor will raise his daughters on his own, in his 'country' that stops at the perimeter of his property.

He is willing to pay property taxes, and other fees necessary to keep utilities going, and these can be deducted from his bank account.

No one will trespass on his property. When his youngest daughter is 18, they will surely be grown and properly educated in his values, and they will be able to face the nasty world that America has become.

Anyone who violates the borders of his country will be shot, with the exception of the courier who will bring clothes, food and other supplies as needed.

Victor states he has a foolproof plan to bring the supplies into the house, without exposing himself to hostile fire.

The girls will be allowed to play in the backyard, but not go beyond it. He has installed an 'invisible fence' and will put collars on them so they will not try to leave the property. "I know that sounds bad. Once they are educated, I will take the collar off. They will understand I will shoot them if they try to leave without my permission. I'll do anything to protect them from the evils of this world."

He really makes no demands, other than "Go away, leave us alone. Don't come in here."

6 – Psychological Consultation

This man is all about control. If you try to control him, he will almost surely escalate. Therefore, be careful about cutting off water, electricity or the like, as this will be perceived, even more than most subjects, as an attack.

He will certainly object to the appearance of police and SWAT, in particular.
- Simply respond in a matter-of-fact way that he is a professional, and there should be no surprise at the response of police.
- He may be dismissive or disrespectful of SWAT. Simply recognize his special talent and history and deflect by saying that you are following standard procedure, but he knows full well as long as there is no danger to the children, SWAT will not be required to act. Rather, you intend to continue speaking with him, in mutual respect, in order to figure a way to resolve this situation for the benefit of his daughters.

Maintain a formal tone. Do not speak to him as a buddy: be neither friendly nor casual. His self-image demands he be taken seriously. Remember, too, he is not 'fronting' as to how dangerous he is. He clearly is a paranoid, psychologically disturbed individual, but he has been among the best warfighters America has produced.

Try not, however, to focus on his war history. Rather, it may prove to be productive to speak about his work trying to mitigate the death penalty. It is possible something occurred in this work that has changed his attitude towards society and his place in it (for example, someone whom he believes is innocent was executed, despite evidence that the trial was unfair, or evidence was mishandled).

Get him talking about his daughters, trying to find out where he perceives them as resilient. Validate his concerns about their mothers' parenting, but only in so far as stating that you understand these are HIS concerns. The goal is going to be his coming to a viewpoint that his daughters are resilient enough to withstand the onslaught of modern, superficial culture.

It is possible that you may be able to link this to how the Roma withstood being absorbed within mainstream culture, but you must ascertain first what his attitude is towards his people. Remember, he married an outsider, and anyway, the cultural values of the Roma are about as far from an American military special operations unit as it is possible to get. He may be militantly NOT part of that culture at all. He considers his marriage a mistake; does he consider it a mistake that she was non-Roma?

Do not equate being a police officer to that of the military. He may see the compromises law enforcement officers must do to work within the law as weak, unlike the units he worked with that "made the rules, and only focused on winning."

Do not assume he suffered from his military experience, that he had PTSD, TBI or the like. If you can contact the VA, see what you can find out about this, as it may help to ascertain how impulsive he might be. It will be good practice to actually call the VA, if only to see how long it will take you to find the right resource. Add this information to your resource list.

<u>Call the VA police.</u> They have records of crimes committed while in the military that will not, necessarily, become part of an ordinary criminal history.

Honor and control is the access route with this man. He will have to feel, at least in some manner, that he has established more control over his daughters' lives in surrendering. Of course, he will not get custody, but is it possible he could receive a promise his daughters will be fed and clothed more to his values, and "whatever happens when this incident is over," you will be able to have some input in how they grow up." This type of 'concession,' however, can only be brought up well into the negotiation, when he is convinced you respect and understand his sense of honor, even though you do not approve of what he's done.

Incorporation of SWAT in Scenario 6

This could be set up so that due to an impasse or escalation, SWAT must enter the house. This could be an incredibly challenging training scenario—the role player could, in this case, be an 'operator' or SWAT. There could be three adults or youth of small stature in the house to play the daughters, or at least life-size human figures, if the training scenario might present danger ('flashbangs,' SIMS, etc).

This exercise could be set up for low-light conditions, booby-traps or any one of another set of conditions that fully train SWAT in a way that is a logical outcome of the HNT scenario.

SCENARIO 6 – Checklist for After Action Review

The after action assessment/critique will depend on what was expressed and expected of the team going into the exercise. In other words, what was the desired training goal or outcome? Not just the outcome of the scenario, but what are the skills the director (team leader) is hoping to see exercised by the team, as these scenarios/situations develop?

Establish floor plan
- ❑ Did not meet goal
- ❑ Partially met goal
- ❑ Fully met goal

Engage or consider assistance from DV detective/unit
- ❑ Did not meet goal
- ❑ Partially met goal
- ❑ Fully met goal

Practice or collect contact information for veteran's assistance
- ❑ Did not meet goal
- ❑ Partially met goal
- ❑ Fully met goal

Demonstrate good listening skills
- ❑ Did not meet goal
- ❑ Partially met goal
- ❑ Fully met goal

SCENARIO 7

Aggressive Borderline Personality

7 – Original Call – Summary

Possible domestic violence (DV). Neighbor calling, stating she hears yelling and the sound of breaking dishes, and the words, "Shut up, mom, or I will shoot you dead" Officers respond, and two subjects inside scream for them to go away, with one threatening to shoot. Officers backed off, and requested SWAT and HNT.

7 – The Incident: Call and First-Responder Contact

Terry, age twenty-four, lives with his mother. The next-door neighbor, one of Terry's mom's best friends, called police after hearing an argument between mother and son. She's heard yelling and breaking dishes before, but this time she heard Terry yell, "You shut up, mom, or I will shoot you dead." Since then, it's been silent.

Police went to the door and knocked, and Terry screamed, "Get the fuck away or I'll start shooting."

His mother yells, "Do as he says! This fucking kid has a gun, and he's lucky he does, cause I'd kick his ass otherwise."

Terry yells, "Shut the fuck up mom! Shut up! Shut up! Shut up!"

His mother yells, "Seriously, you dudes should get off my porch, or this kid is going to shoot someone. And I don't want it to be me! I can talk to this little fucker . . ."

"SHUT UP MA!"

". . .but not with you guys on the porch."

Police yell they are pulling back.

7 – Background for the Role Player

Terry's life has gone to hell. He was a stagehand, but while setting up the scenery for a Shakespeare play, one of the lights, improperly secured, fell from about twenty feet. He was bent over at the time and it hit him in the lumbar spine. Although not disabled, he has been in constant pain. He has a lawsuit going against the theatre, but they deny responsibility because they'd contracted with an outside company to do the set-up, and Terry was one of their employees. The company, on the other hand, claims they were ordered to use the equipment of the theatre, some of which, including the lighting, was substandard. While they litigate, Terry has been left in limbo.

Terry will give this information in rants to the police and will mention the name of the theater group.

7 – Interview with Neighbor

Mrs. Arnold, Terry's mother, aged 62, is a tough woman who bartends at a biker bar. She doesn't take any grief from anyone, but the neighbor says she frequently does over-the-fence complaining about her son. She says she hates his life-style and worries that he drinks far too much.

Terry has kind of a punk persona. He's got multiple piercings, and his mother says he has made two previous alleged suicide attempts.

He overdosed on Fentanyl patches he stole from his grandmother, while she was dying of cancer about four years ago. Last year, during an argument with his boyfriend, he tried to drive into a bridge abutment, but the boyfriend managed to yank the steering wheel straight. "And would you believe it, he bragged to his mother they went home and had the best sex in weeks!"

7 – Call to Terry's Counselor:

The counselor will be standoffish, and will want to argue with the interviewer about client-therapist confidentiality. He will refuse to talk.

The team needs to quickly research the laws regarding confidentiality in life-threatening situations, call the counselor again, and cite the law and demand information. The counselor will be resentful, will complain s/he feels like s/he is betraying his/her client, but will give only the information you directly ask for.

The counselor will inform you that he is diagnosed with a borderline personality disorder. Terry has made multiple slashes on his wrists, but denies he wanted to die. He says he was "just getting the poison out," and pointing to his pierced lip, eyebrow, nose and multiple rings on his ear, said, "it's just more of the same."

Regarding the two actual suicide attempts, the counselor relays Terry tends to be "a little impulsive."

The counselor will be protective of Terry, and will allude to concerns police will be violent to Terry based on his alternative lifestyle.

The counselor will try to terminate the call as quickly as possible, saying, "This is really out of my comfort zone. I feel like I'm being forced to betray Terry here."

Incorporation of members of a local mental health agency

This is a good scenario to invite participation from a local mental health agency. If there is an agency in your jurisdiction that your team might potentially have contact with, see if they would be interested in participating in this exercise with you. Often, positive relationships are developed out of cross trainings like this. Mental health workers rarely get to see the 'inside' workings of law enforcement, and when they do, they usually find it fascinating. If you can elicit the agency's co-operation, and ask a member to play the part of the counselor, perhaps, allow them to observe the rest of the exercise, it could pay huge dividends for the future.

7 –Initial Contact – For the Role Player

Negotiators establish phone contact. Terry is hyper-emotional. The negotiators should be doing a lot of paraphrasing. Terry will be all over the place, mostly talking about his injury, how much pain he is in, how his mother is a bitch. (The mom, in the background, will yell at him things like, "Watch your mouth!" Terry will escalate, screaming at her). The negotiator is going to have to repeatedly 'reel him back in'.

This will be volatile family crisis, opposed to a clear hostage situation. Terry will make no demands except that the police "get the fuck out." However, he will continue to engage. He'll slam down the phone sometimes, but will pick up when you call again.

7 – Contact with Terry's Friend

If the team is listening, they will notice repeated references to a theater group. If the group is called, they will get the name of Terry's friend, Amanda. She says Terry just broke up with his boyfriend, Billy. She says, "These guys are not like the kind of gay guys you see in the movies. I mean—they are so macho in their own minds that they don't even want to touch a girl. Only another guy can be with them. They are kinda like punk-Nazis, not like they hate Jews or any of that shit, but that's the kind of attitude they have. They roll on weekends, hitting the bars, and Terry usually talks shit to people who look at him, and he and Billy kick their ass." She says Billy was into 'crystal,' and Terry used as well, but not as much. They copped drugs at his mother's bar."

Amanda says she heard last week, Billy started getting really aggressive, acting like it was a big joke, but coming up behind Terry and grabbing him and doing body drops on their bed. Terry hit his back where it was injured, and it hurt so bad he started to cry. Billy started laughing at him for being a pussy, and Terry grabbed the cat and threw it in Billy's face. Billy got scratched up pretty bad, including a gash in the cornea of one eye. He responded by beating Terry bloody.

They broke up, and the cat is at the vets,' and Billy says Terry owes the medical bills.

Amanda gives Billy's phone number, but warns he doesn't like cops.

7 – Call to Billy

Billy is going to be suspicious and standoffish with the interviewer. It will be up to the interviewer to get some kind of rapport, giving him 'respect,' without sucking up to him.

Billy is going to state he's been clean from drugs since the incident. He will sound 'street,' but also sound sober and logical. He says Terry can be a 'little pussy bitch,' but then he'll shift into blaming himself. "I know Terry is really hurt. Man, that soft tissue damage stuff, nobody believes it's real. Hell, I forgot about it myself and look what happened."

Billy will offer to speak directly to Terry:

"I want to make this right. Let me talk to him. I can get him out. He loves me. You gotta understand; he's a really emotional guy. You say the wrong thing, and he just goes off. Everyone says I'm the crazy one, but I just like to fight sometimes. You know, you get pissed off, and punching someone or getting your own lights punched out, it just makes things simple. Terry, though, he's just so fucking emotional. He reacts before he thinks. I gotta apologize to him anyway and make it good, but like I say, I'm the only one who knows how to talk to him so he doesn't explode."

7 – Commentary on Potential Third Party Intermediary (TPI)

This is a good exercise for a team leader to test the decision-making skills of the team. This can be set up that not only does Billy make the offer, but you can also have Terry make the same demand.

What does the team do? Do they agree to that without much thought or investigation? If so, bring Billy on….and then, gee whiz, Terry kills himself while telling Billy it's all for him.

However, if the team explores this as an option, it might allow them to practice for a potential TPI. Do they thoroughly interview Billy, to determine if he is stable and can be controlled? Do they have equipment that has a 'kill switch' on Billy's mic, if necessary? Have they spent enough time with Terry and investigating Terry's background that they do not believe he is using Billy as an audience to suicide? Or, maybe the team wishes to practice the method of having Billy make a recorded statement that can be played to Terry, something that could be played in a straightforward manner, or the role player could make it make it really challenging. All of these are valuable training options.

On the Use of TPI

The writers are well aware how badly a TPI call can go, and how rare that this is a viable option. However, it is very common that the public believes it is a good idea, and it frequently comes up in court. Family members and their attorneys assert that had they been allowed on the phone, the subject would have absolutely surrendered. One good training exercises for the team is to consider and prepare for TPI in good faith, so that your agency can assert honestly in court that you have the tools if/when it is ever a possibility—and can then assert that through that preparation, it was clearly established that it was NOT a good idea in this case.

The team can also try this and film it, to prepare for a future court case, showing how quickly such an incident can get out of control. With the family member on the phone, yelling, perhaps, at the hostage-takers and amping them up, this could prove a useful illustration were the question is ever to be raised in a lawsuit why the team didn't use family members as TPI. It also would be a good lead-in for SWAT to get practice on entry/taking out the hostage takers and rescuing the hostages.

7 – Psychological Consult

The consultant states although people with borderline personality disorder usually make parasuicidal moves (cutting on themselves, as Terry has), they also do kill themselves in fairly high numbers, usually when swept by heightened emotions.

The most salient point is that whatever Terry feels, he will become. He will 'emotionally' not remember what he felt before. The danger is if the negotiator 'slips:'—by getting too casual, off-hand, or authoritarian, which evokes Terry's anger, he will be explosive. Remember, this is a guy who threw a cat in his boyfriend's face.

The negotiator should stay matter-of-fact, like a solid uncle or aunt with a kid prone to tantrums. The goal is to create a dialogue where, for a sustained period, Terry is calm.

If possible, speak with his mother and tell her to chill out. (Depending on how intense an exercise you wish to create, the mother can either be accepting or belligerent, which will amp things up again).

SCENARIO 7– Checklist for After Action Review

The after action assessment/critique will depend on what was expressed and expected of the team going into the exercise. In other words, what was the desired training goal or outcome? Not just the outcome of the scenario, but what are the skills the director (team leader) is hoping to see exercised by the team, as these scenarios/situations develop?

Established floor plan
- ❏ Did not meet goal
- ❏ Partially met goal
- ❏ Fully met goal

Demonstrated listening skills
- ❏ Did not meet goal
- ❏ Partially met goal
- ❏ Fully met goal

Demonstrated knowledge regarding HIPAA ("Health Insurance Portability and Accountability Act") laws to deal with therapists, etc.
- ❏ Did not meet goal
- ❏ Partially met goal
- ❏ Fully met goal

How well did the team deal with the idea of using a TPI?
- ❏ Did not meet goal
- ❏ Partially met goal
- ❏ Fully met goal

SCENARIO 8

Psychosis

This scenario, connected to #7, should be assumed to be three months subsequent.

8 – Call to Local Crisis Line

Billy calls the local crisis line. (This could be a valuable training exercise for the interface between the crisis line and 9-1-1. You can have the role-player actually call the crisis line—of course, the counselor is aware that this is a training exercise, but crisis line should carry out the exercise while also continuing with business-as-usual, eventually patching the call to 9-1-1).

Billy rambles, not making much sense. The crisis line staff initially believes they are talking with a psychotic individual, delusional, who is reaching out for someone to talk to, kind of a link to the outside world. However, as the call progresses, he keeps alluding to a 'child of purity' who must be sacrificed to God at the appointed hour (nine hours after whatever time you are starting the exercise).

8 – Patch to 9-1-1

The crisis line patches the call to 9-1-1, and they do a successful trace. Not so coincidentally, communications and the same police sector/district, where the psychotic caller is, have been working for the last 30 minutes on a report of a missing child, an eleven-year-old boy named Spencer Douglas. His mother has not seen him in hours. He lives down the street from Billy.

8 – Original Call, Roughly Simultaneous to Call to Crisis Line

In the call from 9-1-1 to first responders, they provide the concurrent information of a missing child search, and it could be related to a caller who called the crisis line from Billy's address.

Officers are dispatched to Billy's home, where he shows himself in an upstairs window, with a gun to Spencer's head. He yells at them to leave, that the hour of grace has not arrived, "We will all wait until the appointed hour." (Now eight hours from this contact time). Officers request SWAT and HNT.

8 – Contact with the 9-1-1 Call Taker who took the call over from Crisis Line

"He talked all over the place. He said he was assaulted with a lynx, ripping his face with tiger claws, and how his silvery glittery best friend, whose face used to shine in the lights of the city, wanted to kill his mother. He kept asking, 'Are you taping this call? Why did you want to talk to me,' even though he called them."

"He said he knew how to make his face heal, that the blood of a 'child of purity' would make him clean."

8 – Interview with Friend

If you have used Scenario 7, and Terry 'survived,' you can have the interview with Terry, who will be hyper-dramatic, shifting between fronting macho toughness, complaints about his own problems, and anger at Billy. If you wish to have your negotiators receive the information more painlessly, the informant can simply be a rational friend who reports:

Billy has been tweaking for months. Ever since the hostage situation with Terry and his mother, his solution to the problem was to buy a lot of methamphetamine and do it continuously,

"Billy thinks crystal meth is the best thing in the world. I was with him the first time he used, and he took the hit and he shook himself and said, 'I'm finally home",

"He crashes hard. He gets so depressed—and his solution to depression is to get pissed off. If he can target anyone, he has a focus and a purpose that pushes the depression to the background,

Ever since he broke up with Terry, he's been keeping to himself. There's no one to target, but what's in his brain. The dude is really paranoid."

8 – Interview with Billy's Father

Finding collateral contacts

Determine how we are going to find Billy's father. Is he in town or out of state? Find innovative ways to have your team practice using the Internet and all information means necessary to locate people. (It is likely that Billy has a Facebook page) If you have someone on your team who is computer savvy, enlist their assistance in coming up with good ideas for developing information resources. Hostage Negotiations Teams usually have one or two people who are excellent at researching on the Internet. The team comes to rely on them. This becomes a problem when you have a call out, and those individuals are not available. Anytime you can cross-train team members, and develop more skills for Intel discovery, the more coverage the team will have.

The father recalls two episodes of psychosis in Billy's teen-years, periods of about five months each where he hallucinated, and heard voices. These preceded his drug use.

Billy's father also informs police that a security guard at the mall sexually molested Billy when he was twelve years old. He had been shoplifting and the guard grabbed him. He threatened him with arrest and prison and told Billy there was a way to make it good—if Billy just did a little favor for him. Billy's dad first heard about this when Billy was fifteen, during his first psychotic break.

The father went to the mall, asking questions about the security guard, but he had died two years previously at a Costco, when one of the pallets being loaded on a top shelf slipped off the forklift. The guard had ignored the yellow tape and just happened to be in the wrong place at the wrong time.

Billy refused to talk about the abuse ever again, but has had a strong hostility towards law enforcement, particularly anyone in uniform.

8 – Initial Contact

Ascertain the sex of the security guard who raped him. This is one of those cases where gender concerns matter. It may be helpful, if it is possible, to use a negotiator of the gender opposite to that of the rapist.

- When you ask about the child's well-being, Billy will tell you he's perfect, everything is fine, and he will be in God's arms soon, after he heals Billy's wounds.
- If you ask how he will heal the wounds, Billy will reply, "with his bubbling blood."
- Every time you try to get Billy more coherent, or focused on Spencer's well-being, he will become more psychotic.
- He will be very suspicious and hostile to the police. He can raise the subject of the negotiation in #7, regarding his ex-boyfriend, Terry.

The director should make this role-player aware of the outcome of #7. It should be 'bad,' regardless. Either Terry survived, and he broke up with Billy, or he killed himself or was shot by police.

- If Billy was used as a TPI in the previous exercise, he will blame himself for either the break-up or Terry's death.
- If they wouldn't allow Billy to speak to Terry, the outcome will be the fault of the police.

Remember, however, for the sake of this exercise, we want to focus the officer's skills on communicating with a psychotic individual. Furthermore, the well-being of the child is paramount. It will be important that the negotiator does not get distracted about the past incident/scenario, particularly if it amps Billy up. And finally, given that he is psychotic, Billy will be all over the place. The negotiator's task is to get him to focus. It will be essential to get a psych consult as soon as possible in this situation, to most effectively communicate with this man.

8 – Psych Consult Concerning Psychotic, Delusional Subjects

Try to divert his attention from the child. You certainly can make the attempt to suggest he let the child go, but if this does not work, try to get Billy communicating with you about himself. This may give the child a chance to escape, and furthermore, it fixes Billy in one place.

He will seem incoherent, talking in images and word pictures. Try to help him get clearer by <u>paraphrasing</u> your understanding of what he's saying. Keep it very simple. If he says, "A lynx with its glittery spangly claws ripped my face off," respond with a statement, (NOT a question), such as "Something hurt your face." <u>Make anything complex he says as simple as you can in paraphrase.</u>

Notice any areas of his speech where he seems to clear up, and is less delusional or even focused and coherent. These are called <u>islands of sanity.</u> Divert your contact to those 'islands of sanity,' whenever possible, rather than allowing the conversation to focus on delusional subjects. Make links with other subjects not tainted by delusions. Think of yourself as expanding the size of the 'land-mass of the island,' making an area where it's predictable and safe. If Terry gets stuck within his delusions, you may find changing the subject requires real finesse. Nonetheless, do so whenever you can, because talking about delusions makes it worse.

Do not agree with his delusions. You don't know where he's going with them. You may agree with him and find out you've confirmed, for him, the sacrifice of the child.

Do your best not to argue with him. The problem, of course, is he is fixed on sacrificing Spencer to heal his wounds. Although not an argument, you can suggest, "There is another way." Offer something benign, like broken leaves of aloe or sage smoke . . . Aside from the hope he might agree to let the child go, you are continuing the dialogue, which will give SWAT more time to get into position.

Do tell Billy although you don't perceive what he does, you aren't arguing with them about what *he* sees or believes. However, because his delusion is murderous, you must be very careful here. Try to steer him to more 'solid ground.' For example, "I believe you were wounded. It sounds bad. I'd like you to come out here so our medic can take a look at it." OR "I believe you are wounded. I heard you were clawed by your own cat. Your friend told me your cat is at the vet. It'd be good if you went and checked how she is doing."

SCENARIO 8 – Checklist for After Action Review

The after action assessment/critique will depend on what was expressed and expected of the team going into the exercise. In other words, what was the desired training goal or outcome? Not just the outcome of the scenario, but what are the skills the director (team leader) is hoping to see exercised by the team, as these scenarios/situations develop?

Established a floor plan?
- ❏ Did not meet goal
- ❏ Partially met goal
- ❏ Fully met goal

Intel demonstrated knowledge/use of social media/internet to develop Intel
- ❏ Did not meet goal
- ❏ Partially met goal
- ❏ Fully met goal

Did team locate the father in a reasonable amount of time? Using realistic means?
- ❏ Did not meet goal
- ❏ Partially met goal
- ❏ Fully met goal

Did primary negotiator, coach negotiator, or other team member catch on to gender issue regarding gender of rapist?
- ❏ Did not meet goal
- ❏ Partially met goal
- ❏ Fully met goal

Did gender of negotiator come into consideration?
- ❏ Did not meet goal
- ❏ Partially met goal
- ❏ Fully met goal

Would it be important to have psych consult on this one? Was one called?
- ❏ Did not meet goal
- ❏ Partially met goal
- ❏ Fully met goal

How did team deal with the delusional behavior?
- ❏ Did not meet goal
- ❏ Partially met goal
- ❏ Fully met goal

SCENARIO 9

School Hostage Situation:
Is He an Outcast or a Sociopath?

9 – Original Call

Armed student at the high school. Possible hostage situation. Caller is a faculty member calling from the main office. Officers respond, contain the school, and are able to contain the classroom. No known shots fired. SWAT and HNT enroute immediately.

9 – Incident

Jeremy, a high school sophomore walked into a senior English class, armed with a handgun. He ordered some children and the teacher to leave. He currently has seven hostages, four boys and three girls. The only thing similar about the kids is they are all 'popular,' whom other kids think are elite. No shots were fired, nor were any kids hurt. He did strike the teacher across the face with the handgun, making a deep gouge on the teacher's cheekbone. The teacher, in a gentle voice, was trying to reassure Jeremy his problems, whatever they were, could be worked out. Jeremy said to him after he hit him, "Don't you patronize me. Don't you fucking talk down to me."

9 – Joint Interview with a Teacher and a Guidance Counselor

The negotiators are going to (or should) interview all the children as well as the one teacher who were all released from the classroom. In addition to asking about the mental state, and background of Jeremy, the negotiators are going to be asking about the layout of the room, windows, possible weapons he could use, things he could use to barricade the doors or make booby traps with. These are all things the director needs to have prepared in advance, and either 'coach' role players (if you have the luxury of having that many bodies to actually play living subjects), or have prepared on sheets of paper to offer up as 'information sheets' when the negotiators ask the right questions. Remember, the other alternative is to have a designated 'information person' who will be the one person who plays all the roles of the potential interviews. This person does not necessarily have to be a good actor, but need to provide information when the negotiators ask the right questions, or explain where they would go to request/locate information. (For example, "The janitor says there is a large vent in the room where the incident is happening, and teachers in classroom #7 complain that you can actually hear conversations from the incident room.") The director/team leader really should not be this person, as they should be paying attention to many other things, and watching the process as a whole, and really cannot be focused enough to be this person. A scenario like this one may have many potential witnesses that must be interviewed.

With this many informants, there will be a lot of 'noise' compared to message. The first informants, teachers and a few students will tell you that he is a loner, he has been picked on, shoved into lockers, ostracized, etc. It is not major torment, but teachers think he is somewhat bullied.

9 – Initial Contact by Negotiator

Jeremy is quite willing to talk on the classroom phone. Initial interviews with the freed kids say he is very calm, says he won't hurt anyone.

Given the information provided, the negotiator will naturally assume you have a bullied kid, who will present with high emotions. Jeremy will be agitated in the beginning of the call so standard operating procedures will seem in order. Paraphrasing, trying to draw him out. However, after a period of time, things will stalemate. Jeremy will not give the negotiator any explicit demands, and subtly, after a period of time, he will begin to twist the negotiators words, becoming argumentative.

You will hear him making threats towards the hostages in the background, followed by promises and reassurances, then more threats. If the negotiator is paying attention s/he will note that Jeremy seems to be in control rather than out of control.

9 – Directions to the Role Player

This could be a difficult role for you to play. In the beginning, you will complain of being pushed around in school. Remember the kind of grievances just about any kid had about the 'popular kids' (even a lot of the popular kids have the same grievances.)

After about one half hour, one of the hostages will start begging to be let go. Promise you will, and then take back the promise. Then promise again.

Then begin to subtly mess with the negotiator. Misunderstand what he or she is saying. Become a little argumentative. Play dumb. Distort what they say. Laugh at the wrong time.

After about forty-five minutes, hang up the phone, saying you will be talking to them in about ten minutes, but you need a break. As a good faith gesture, let go one of the hostages, but do so in a way that is demeaning; make them go out without their shirt, or with only one pant leg on or underwear on their head. (This must be something that is prearranged before the exercise, out of respect for the role player!).

It will be after this that the police will be interviewing the students and getting a better idea of your character.

9 – Student Interviews

Other students have asked to talk to the negotiators in private, and they raise new concerns. Negotiators will have already noticed his presentation on the phone wasn't congruent with a pushed-around bullied kid. Students admit they sometimes do push him around, but that Jeremy was not a victim. Boys pushed him after he whispered vile obscenities near their girlfriends. He would pick someone out and stare at them, with a little smile on his face, but would break it off just before it got so intimidating or unpleasant that the student would tell the teacher. Further questioning from the police seems to show he picked the kind of kids to intimidate who would probably not tell anyone in authority.

Kids said they were scared of him. One girl said she and her girl friends used to call him The Nightstalker, because he 'creeped' them out so much.

9 – Psychological/Tactical Consult

Do not explicitly let on that you know he is such a master manipulator. This has become a game of chess, and you need to be just a little bit ahead of him. Because he is an aggressive narcissist, you will ideally induce him to release some of the hostages, as if it's his idea.

Throughout this exercise, he will release several hostages in exchange for something. Do NOT play power-games, for example, he asks for a pizza for himself and the hostages and you say you can just get him burgers.

> **REMEMBER, you do not know, for sure, if he intends to kill the hostages or what his motivation is. (For this reason, SWAT could easily be integrated into this exercise, turning it into an active shooter scenario, with the negotiator's function to keep him in one place and not aware of what's happening around him).**

The negotiator should definitely hone into what Jeremy wants. The negotiator could use the usual tactic of suggesting that although this could develop in a bad situation, it's not yet. He's still a minor, he's a smart, articulate guy, and he should be able to explain his situation to people. Emphasize he has his age on his side—NOW—but if he harms the hostages, the courts these days regard him as an adult. (In other words, if he releases the hostages now, he's been smart enough to play to system).

Jeremy's motivation is to have a thrill, and he intends to use the 'bullied kid' image as his excuse and defense. Suggest people will understand if he lets the hostages go now and surrenders. He's made his point. Let him think he's fooled you, that he's played you for fools. Your manipulation is to let him believe he's manipulating you.

Jeremy can be considered an "aggressive narcissist, which is what a sociopath truly is. The only thing that matters is himself. Get him talking about himself. Do not give him obvious praise, but listen in a way that makes him think he has a 'captive audience,' who is impressed with him. With this guy, however, you want to accept his story at face value, unless he abandons it. If you 'bust' him, you've proved you are smarter than he is—remember this: he probably doesn't have a back-up plan beyond the bullied kid approach. Without that, he may decide to put you in your place by hurting the remaining hostages.

What is most dangerous is if you insult him, question his seriousness, or challenge him. He very possibly will take this out on one of the hostages.

This should be regarded as a "victim taking" scenario, not a "hostage taking" situation, as there is really nothing to gain in what he is doing.

Scenario 9 Alternative – Possible Suicide by Cop

This exercise can ALSO end with a suicide-by-cop scenario, after the hostages are released. Narcissists, in particular, often crash after their fantasy is lived out, and he may want to up the ante. He can also retain one or more hostages and SWAT can go 'green-light' and take him out.

SCENARIO 9 – Checklist for After Action Review

The after action assessment/critique will depend on what was expressed and expected of the team going into the exercise. In other words, what was the desired training goal or outcome? Not just the outcome of the scenario, but what are the skills the director (team leader) is hoping to see exercised by the team, as these scenarios/situations develop?

Floor plan established?
- ❏ Did not meet goal
- ❏ Partially met goal
- ❏ Fully met goal

How did team handle interviews with released hostages?
- ❏ Did not meet goal
- ❏ Partially met goal
- ❏ Fully met goal

Did the primary demonstrate good listening skills?
- ❏ Did not meet goal
- ❏ Partially met goal
- ❏ Fully met goal

How did the primary deal with the threats?
- ❏ Did not meet goal
- ❏ Partially met goal
- ❏ Fully met goal

How was this situation status discussed with the command post? Options?
- ❏ Did not meet goal
- ❏ Partially met goal
- ❏ Fully met goal

SCENARIO 10

Fetal Alcohol or Other Conditions that Cause
Cognitive and Emotional Limitations

Making the Event as Realistic as Possible

With proper coaching, and the use of such safety equipment as SIRT® (laser) pistols and mock Tasers, this entire initial scene could be role-played. (Simunitions® and the like require masks, which makes communication unnatural—thus we recommend that the team use SIRT® pistols, if possible).

First responders can get practice at the control of irate family members, and shoot/no-shoot decision making with the armed father. The role players in this case can be police or well-coached civilians, to prevent the father's behavior from going over the line creating a shoot situation.

---

10 – Original Call

Report of a disturbance. Complainant states people are out in the yard, and that they hear yelling and screaming. They believe it is a domestic disturbance, and one man might be armed with a gun. Officers respond.

Police arrive at the residence, and observe a man, a woman and two kids engaged in an argument. The man is holding a weapon that he initially refuses to put down. He almost gets shot. The father is very argumentative with police, yelling about his child—but initially, he's too incoherent for the officers to understand what he's upset about. Two other children are screaming, and mother was yelling at them and at the father.

When the situation is finally stabilized, the police are informed that there is a third child, held hostage in her bedroom inside the house.

What they then learn is: A man climbed into what he thought was an empty house, but there was a family of five sleeping there. He walked into the bedroom, found the parents sleeping, and surprised, yelled, "Ah, shit."

Dad woke up, grabbed a gun which he keeps beside the bed and began firing. He emptied an entire magazine of 18 rounds, which went everywhere, but missed the intruder. One bullet went through the ceiling and through their son's bed, missing the sleeping boy by a foot. Two other rounds went out the bedroom down a hallway, out a window and into the neighbor's house.

The intruder panicked and ran upstairs. He entered the bedroom of the younger of the two daughters, Brittany, aged seven. He locked the door, and began barricading it with furniture.

Father reloaded, intending to pursue him and shoot him down. His wife managed to catch him at the door, and smacked him upside the head, ordering him to help her clear the house with the other kids and call the cops. The intruder yelled he would "kill the kid if anyone comes in. Just leave me alone. Leave me alone." According to the wife, his voice sounded both angry and scared.

They left the house, with the father still armed, and they then began arguing on the front lawn, at which point the police arrived.

HNT and SWAT are called. HNT is able to set up communication. The subject identifies himself as Trey Conroy. A criminal background check shows a history of impulsive crimes, burglaries and substance abuse. He does not have a history of severe violence, but he has several simple assaults on his record.

For the director, you will need to invent the full ID, and criminal history for Trey. If you elicit the assistance of your communications personnel, they are usually happy to assist in generating realistic looking computer hits/police reports, court orders, etc, if you wish to make it as realistic as possible. Of course, if your resources and time are limited, you do need to have all this information in the hands of the 'information person' who will deliver it to the negotiators, when the time and opportunity comes for them to discover it (i.e., if they have followed the appropriate leads).

10 – Interview with Trey's Friends

Trey's mother was a serious alcoholic. She drank throughout her pregnancy. Trey was born with fetal alcohol syndrome. He is currently 26 years old.

He is a small man, kind of skinny, but physically strong. His friends used to say he had 'freaky monkey strength,' which came in handy because they used him to rob houses. He can climb up the gutter or façade of a house as easily as a chimp. His buddies have straightened up their lives, but Trey still engages in stupid unplanned crimes. They say that Trey is really volatile with women, because he thinks they are always laughing at him.

An Added Factor: 'Gender Volatility'

This should be a caution to the team in selecting a lead negotiator. If a female negotiator is the lead, let them get an hour or so practice, with some success, but eventually, Trey should get so volatile with her (merely because she is a woman) that it should be clear you will need to change negotiators. (This is be discussed in the AAR, so it is clear to the first lead this was programmed into the exercise and not a failure on the negotiator's part).

NOTE 2: The 'gender volatility' could be reversed as well, so that Trey is aggressive towards men whom he thinks are putting him down or something similar.

10 – Contact with Mother

Mom is suspicious and drunk and it will take some time to convince her they need information to help her son. Finally she says he has a small handgun, a.25 caliber Colt. It is a collector's item she wanted to sell, but he hid it in a leaky shed behind her house, which rusted it so badly that the collector who had been willing to pay her $500 withdrew his offer. She will get sidetracked, because she's angry with him for letting the gun get damaged, so that she didn't get the money. When asked if she knows if the gun works, she'll say, "Hell I don't know. I used to tell him, 'Here's the only thing I ever got from your father except you. Too bad he didn't shoot blanks. I don't know about his gun, though." She thinks this is very funny.

10 – Negotiation

Negotiation will be difficult. Trey is quite emotional, panicked, and he will not track the information the officers try to give him. At one moment, he seems amenable to giving up, but he takes offense at something the officers say, and becomes threatening, hysterical or simply cuts off the call. If the negotiator uses complicated sentences or big words, Trey will get angry, because he won't understand and think the officer is doing it deliberately to make him feel stupid.

10 – Psychological Consult

The psychology department of the local university is contacted, and one professor, an expert on Fetal Alcohol Syndrome, gives them more data. The problem, he says, is such individuals have a much less sophisticated neurological organization. "It's not that he is intellectually disabled in the ordinary sense. When he learns something, however, it is stored 'locally.' In other words, the filing system is limited and it's hard to access the information if, for example, his mood changes. If you use complicated language, he will think you are "making him stupid," and impulsively lash out to make you stop. On the other hand, he will be very sensitive to being talked down to. Unlike intellectually disabled folks (those who used to be designated as mentally retarded), who can be childlike, Trey is probably a full adult—albeit one who is socially immature and very emotional, and who will easily take offence if he thinks you are trying to make him confused or feel stupid. Your task will be to talk to him in a matter-of-fact way, and be very sensitive to when he is 'not tracking you. One sign of this is he will go silent (he'll be trying to figure out what you said and when he can't, he'll start brooding and become resentful, and eventually will explode into rage).

Clarify any misunderstandings immediately. Be careful, however, that you don't do this in such a way he thinks you are implicitly saying, "This is simple. Any fool can understand this."

SCENARIO 10 – Checklist for After Action Review

The after action assessment/critique will depend on what was expressed and expected of the team going into the exercise. In other words, what was the desired training goal or outcome? Not just the outcome of the scenario, but what are the skills the director (team leader) is hoping to see exercised by the team, as these scenarios/situations develop?

Establish a floor plan
- ❏ Did not meet goal
- ❏ Partially met goal
- ❏ Fully met goal

Background etc. collected in a timely manner
- ❏ Did not meet goal
- ❏ Partially met goal
- ❏ Fully met goal

Did the team recognize what they were dealing with?
- ❏ Did not meet goal
- ❏ Partially met goal
- ❏ Fully met goal

Consider psych consult? Request one?
- ❏ Did not meet goal
- ❏ Partially met goal
- ❏ Fully met goal

Demonstrate good listening skills
- ❏ Did not meet goal
- ❏ Partially met goal
- ❏ Fully met goal

SCENARIO 11

Sexual Exploitation of Adolescent, Narcissism

11 – Original Call

Meet the woman who believes her 14-year-old daughter has been abused by her martial arts teacher. Daughter is in the company of the suspect at this time. Meet the complainant at this location, near the suspect's residence. They request SWAT and HNT.

11 – Interview with First Responders

Ms. Albeniz, a divorced mother of three children called police after confronting her daughter, Esther, aged fourteen, about an intimate relationship the latter is having with her martial arts instructor. Esther claims they are meant for each other. Esther ran out of the house and went to Carl's home. Mom called police, but when they go to the house, Carl briefly appears at the door, wearing his martial arts uniform, with a sword in his hand, and tells them to leave. "This will be solved in the only way possible to preserve my honor and that of my teachers." (Carl is an American—whatever the race of the role player—not a Japanese citizen).

11 – Interview with Ms. Albeniz

About a year ago, Carl was accused of improper contact with then thirteen-year-old Esther, one of his students. She and her mother, Mrs. Albeniz, were taking aikido class together. Apparently, whether by design or 'just something happened,' Carl began to get obsessed with this girl. She was having trouble in school, and he was very encouraging. Her mother, divorced, with three children, was grateful for the interest that Carl gave her daughter. Because of work and family responsibilities, mom soon discontinued training, but encouraged her daughter to continue to go to practice. What she was not aware of is that Carl would cancel practice for the other students because "something came up," and once or twice a month, have a private lesson with Esther.

Esther began acting like a young teenager in love. She got a poster from a martial arts demo Carl did, and put it in her room. After writing "Sensei and Esther forever" all over her notebook, her mother got concerned, and asked her daughter questions about what was going on. As soon as she heard about the private lessons, she called police and a well-done forensic interview took place. As best as could be determined, Carl had been grooming her for over a year, and contact had progressed from understanding and encouragement to isolation ("I understand. No one else does") to comforting embraces to, and this is ambiguous, embraces through her clothes where he 'accidentally' touched areas of her body that are out of bounds. Esther isn't sure about this, however. Esther felt that she betrayed her best friend (and in her mind, future husband). She was furious at her mother for making a big thing about nothing. No charges were pressed, but Esther was taken out of the dojo, and Carl was told to stay away from her.

Today mom found out Carl had met with Esther on a number of occasions. Checking her daughter's diary, she read, "No one understands our love. We will be together. He promises me." When she confronted her daughter, Esther ran to Carl's house.

11 – Follow-up with the Investigator (Police)

This is another opportunity for the HNT to work with the detective who handles these kinds of cases. The director can plan ahead of time with the detective, so all the information and background necessary for the scenario can come out. Carl was interviewed, and confessed to "making a mistake." He maintained he showed "poor judgment," but "nothing really bad happened, and nothing was going to happen. What kind of a guy do you think I am?" He pointed out how mature Esther is, both in body and soul, and "yes, I admit it, maybe I did something that could have confused her, I feel bad about it, really bad," but that he had not done anything illegal. "Let's say, just for discussion, while I was practicing with her, and showing her a throw, my technique wasn't exactly precise and instead of my hand going directly under her arm, I might have brushed across her front— this could easily have happened if she moved incorrectly. I'm not saying it did, but just for an example."

Carl was released on $20,000 bond. Eventually, charges were not pressed. His students took over his dojo, firing him as chief instructor (he was hired rather than owning the place. No one has seen him in months).

11 – Contact with Carl—For the Role Player

Familiarize yourself somewhat with aikido—there is tons of information online about this martial art. Your presentation should be patronizing and stilted; at times, make yourself sound like a bad samurai movie character.

You will be:

- Easily offended, at which point you will talk about your honor as a warrior
- Patronizing to the negotiator. You'll question police tactics—"You only know the language of opposition and force, whereas in aikido, we redirect negative energy to a peaceful resolution" (you will be too full of yourself to see the irony here).
- If you've done your Internet study well, you can talk about O-sensei, the saintly, white-bearded founder of the art, who had super-human powers and proclaimed, "Martial arts are love."
- When you do talk about Esther, you will talk about her as someone who only desires the best for herself—which means, bonding with you. You will talk about her in dismissive terms, as a disciple rather than an equal. If the negotiator talks too long about Esther, get offended and somehow redirect the conversation back to yourself
- You will never make an explicit suicide threat, unless the negotiator threatens you in some way— rather, make allusive statements suggesting that your honor will be served.
- 'Kindly' warn the negotiator not to send in the police, because your sword skills are deadly, and you do not wish to have to resort to unseemly violence.

11 – Interview with Carl's Assistant Instructor

Carl is a teacher of aikido, a martial art claiming to reconcile conflict by redirecting negative forces. It tends to draw people not interested in fighting as much as a more philosophical approach—moral improvement, spiritual development, etc. Which means it's ripe ground for guru types. Nonetheless, Carl has been doing this for about 35 years, and he is a really powerful guy, as well as skilled with the aikido weapons curriculum. They practice with swords and staffs. The assistant instructor will blather on about energy and the moral forces of the universe, and how he cannot believe Carl could ever do anything bad, but "Appearances are everything these days, so we had to let him go. We hoped it would all blow over after awhile, and he could come back and lead us." He will speak of him in idolizing terms. He clearly states Carl is really effective with a sword, and practices cutting bamboo wrapped in straw mats to emulate the structure of the human body. He once cut a bundle of five of these, winning some sort of 'sword cutting tournament.'

11 – Contact with Carl's Own Teacher

At the suggestion of the dojo assistant, a phone call is made to Carl's teacher, Mr. Lockhardt, or "You can call me Sensei." He's a pompous ass. He will discount the gravity of the charges against Carl, saying when he trained in Japan, no one would make a big deal over something like this—a teacher mentoring a student was always considered an honor. Anyway, if the teacher was tempted to stray a bit, it was understood that the student, for the good of the teachers' mission, would either simply withdraw from the school, or if not, realize she was fortunate the teacher was kind enough to give her attention.

The interviewer should feel free to be a cop here. He or she must underscore that a serious crime is being committed at this moment—kidnapping, to be precise—and the nature of Lockhardt's replies cause concern to arise that he is, in some way, involved.

This interview would be great if it could be conducted with a serious, skilled role player, who may have some real information, but it is covered up in a really obnoxious personality. This would be excellent practice in interviewing skills for any police officer. If the leader/director can find someone to really play this role well, it would challenge any interviewer.

Demanding he cut to the chase, the interviewer should ask for an explanation of Carl appearing at the door, wearing his martial arts uniform, with a sword in his hand, saying, "This will be solved in the only way possible that will preserve my honor and that of my teachers."

If he does ask this, Lockhardt will reply if he has done his job well as Carl's teacher, then of course he means suicide. When the interviewer asks the implications for Esther, Lockhardt states if Carl is a true warrior, he will do whatever it takes to protect Esther from shame, and in our small-minded society, given mentor-student relationships are so unthinkingly condemned, there is only one way to preserve her honor, the same as is required of Carl himself.

11 – Further Interviews with Dojo Members

#1 INTERVIEWEE

Carl is a very talented, very intelligent man, whom many admired. But it always had to be his way. He was easily offended, when people disagreed with him. Furthermore, there had been some financial improprieties regarding dojo funds. Carl was a paid employee according to the business structure, but he treated the dojo as his personal possession. When people confronted him on the money issue, he blew up, accused them of lack of loyalty to their instructor, and said, "In olden times, you would deserve death to call your teacher's actions into question." Regrettably, he said, these times were over, but they would never advance in rank in the art again. He allowed them to come to class, but simply ignored them. The three members of the board involved quit.

#2 INTERVIEWEE

"I trust my sensei. There must be an explanation. If the police would just leave him alone, he could solve this problem."

#3 INTERVIEWEE

A female student: "I only lasted six months. The guy always creeped me out. You know the kind of person who is somehow standing too close to you even across the room. His eye contact is too long, and his smile is too fixed. He seems to be listening to everything you say, but eventually you realize he doesn't give a shit. It's all about him."

11 – Consult with an Expert in Japanese Martial Arts

After being told what Lockhardt has said, as well as the members of the school, this long-time former resident of Japan, also an aikido practitioner, states, "That's all crap. Not that the idiot won't kill himself or the child, but there is no specialized mentor-victim relationship like he's describing. These idiots are like the kind of people who read comic books to understand Japan, but they are worse. They just make the whole thing up in their head. At the same time, here's what you need to know about these guys. They believe their own bullshit. They think they are superior and use their little fantasy construct to support whatever it is they do. It's sort of like a cult."

The importance of Intel in developing a psych profile

This is another scenario where the Intel, and development of the psych profile on this guy, is going to be key, for the HNT when they are debriefing the scene commander on what they are facing with Carl. Finding these key potential witnesses are going to be critical. How do you locate that female student who quit the dojo after 6 months? How do you locate the expert on Japanese martial arts (or another culture, if you choose to structure the scenario with another type of martial art)? This is all stuff that needs to be prepared ahead of time, and does require some work on the part of the director, and the team of trainers who are putting on the training. This is why it is beneficial to have a cadre of trainers involved when doing major (even minor) scenario training. If you have a representative from SWAT, communications, investigations, maybe even records division, you can get a whole lot done, and a lot of good ideas for a very realistic training.

11 – Psychological Consult

Take away all the martial arts, and you have a classic narcissist. The task of the negotiator is to get him talking about the most fascinating subject in the whole world to him, himself. You certainly have to check on the well-being of Esther, but be very careful not to put too much energy in this, because, as far as Carl is concerned, this is about him, not her, and he'll get angry. He may become violent or threatening to make you put the attention back on him.

If what your martial arts consultant says is accurate, you have to be careful of a couple of things:
1. He's going to be insecure about his martial arts, because he's probably been accused of being a fraud by others like your consultant.
2. If the negotiator has done combatives or martial arts, do not show too much knowledge, because you have done 'it' for real, as opposed to waving weapons in a dojo. This will make Carl insecure.
3. Carl is similar to a certain B-list movie actor, (a has-been who does aikido, and claimed to teach expert MMA stars how to fight, that he was in the CIA, etc), who always takes great pains to tell others how special he is, and how he is as expert in real life as he is supposed to be in his movies. Carl, like this B-list movie actor, is living in a movie in his head.

If you get him talking a long time about himself, he may start to feel more and more special, smarter than you, or the courts. Support him in minimizing the situation: Esther came over to his house, he probably didn't even invite her, and if this is the misunderstanding it looks like, he should be able to clear it up.

Within limits, express understanding that due to his specialized training, of course he reacted just like his training expected. But he showed control martial artists have—he didn't charge police with his sword, so no one was hurt. (Don't mention it would have been him that got hurt). Thank him for that. Lead him to giving up as a matter of his superior control.

This guy will be really offensive—he will bolster his own ego by putting you down. Be careful not to get your buttons pushed. He will offend you and take offense if you are offended. If you put him in his place like he 'deserves,' he may believe he has to hurt Esther, or at least escalate to prove he is someone who must be taken seriously.

After instructing him on how to surrender, be sure to ask him how his sword should be cared for, if for example, it should be placed in the hands of "Lockhardt sensei", or if he would prefer it cared for in another manner.

11 – The Question of Esther: For a Secondary Role-Player

1. In the basic level scenario training, Esther can be simply quiet, passive
2. To make a more sophisticated exercise, she can get increasingly worried, scared, and there can be by-play between Carl and Esther. If Carl loses his temper, the negotiator should redirect attention on their conversation, away from Esther. Get her on the phone if possible, and not only ask her if she is OK, ask her to be calm so "Carl and I can speak" (he will surely be listening). Of course, try to negotiate her out.

SWAT

1. One opportunity would be if the negotiator can really get Carl involved in pontificating about the wonders of martial arts and enlightened warriors, etc. Esther could appear at the back of the house, at a window and SWAT can practice a rescue of her. At that point, you have a barricaded subject only.
2. If it is so desired, and your role player is fit enough and has some training in combatives, he can attack the officers upon exit, substituting a bamboo kendo stave for a real sword. Depending on the distance, SWAT can practice with less lethal or lethal weapons, as appropriate.

SCENARIO 11 – Checklist for After Action Review

The after action assessment/critique will depend on what was expressed and expected of the team going into the exercise. In other words, what was the desired training goal or outcome? Not just the outcome of the scenario, but what are the skills the director (team leader) is hoping to see exercised by the team, as these scenarios/situations develop?

Floor plan obtained in a timely manner?
- ❏ Did not meet goal
- ❏ Partially met goal
- ❏ Fully met goal

Very important to demonstrate good listening skills
- ❏ Did not meet goal
- ❏ Partially met goal
- ❏ Fully met goal

Allow subject to talk about himself
- ❏ Did not meet goal
- ❏ Partially met goal
- ❏ Fully met goal

Honest status updates to the command post are very important
- ❏ Did not meet goal
- ❏ Partially met goal
- ❏ Fully met goal

SCENARIO 12

Cultural Issues, Suicide as Solution

12 – Original Call

Possible suicide. Subject is on the phone with Crisis line, threatening to kill herself. Subject is on a cell phone. Ping has been placed, and the location is determined to be (location). Officers locate the vehicle, and observe the subject with a firearm. Containment is set up, and a request is made for SWAT and HNT.

12 – Background Information for Role Player

Amira is a bright kid, sixteen years old. She comes from a Pakistani family, who are very devout Muslim. She has one brother and one sister, who have, up to now, done exactly what their parents want them to do. She, too, has tried to be a 'good girl,' wearing hijab, going to the mosque with her parents, and worshiping according to the testaments of their faith.

Her parents have arranged for her to marry a cousin back in Pakistan, someone she has never met. She saw his picture and found him very unattractive. In addition, she wants to be a chemist. She is one of those people who found something that just makes her feel alive. For her, it is chemistry. She feels like she is participating in the clockwork of creation. For her, in joining chemicals together and making compounds, she "knows the heart of Allah, who loves us and wants to bring us together." When the role-player talks about chemistry—or another subject that the role-player is familiar—she should really light up with happiness. This will contrast vividly with her current situation.

Her mother tells her this foolishness must end. She will be a good wife and birth children and that is all there is to it. She has said, "You don't 'fall in love.' That's why so many American's divorce. You do what is good for your family, and after a time, you will find yourself in love with your husband. And if not, the well-being of the family is more important than the feelings of a silly girl."

Furthermore, she has been told, a refusal to marry this young man dishonors the family name. Her brother, at the command of her father, has beaten her, giving her a black eye and multiple bruises on her body.

When she still refuses, and says she will make a scene on the airplane so no one will ever let her fly to Pakistan or anywhere else (she threatened to claim to be a terrorist, if need be), she is told if she continues to shame the family, she is no longer their daughter and they will kill her if that is what it takes to preserve the family's name. All of her family, even her little sister, agree.

12 – Call to the Local Crisis Line

Amira has called a local crisis line in the middle of the night with a cell phone, telling them all of the above information (In the exercise, a role player crisis line counselor should pass the information on to the police. If you inaccurately record this information, you may make a misstep that leads the girl to suicide.

Integration of the Crisis Line in This Scenario

If your jurisdiction has a crisis line, or suicide hot line agency, it might be a good idea to contact them, and see if they would like to participate in this training, by providing a counselor to play him or herself. It is best to do this during working hours, so that the regular business of the crisis line must continue around this role-play incident.

We have found many mental health agencies are more than happy to work with police and cross train, when the opportunities present. When agencies are allowed the opportunity to practice and train with police departments in situations like this, both agencies come out the wiser for it.

She tells the counselor there is no hope for her and she is going to kill herself. When asked why she is calling, she says she just wants someone to understand. She says she has stolen her father's gun and is in a car overlooking the city, watching the city lights. She cannot live like this anymore. When asked if she would be willing to turn the gun over to a police officer, she says she will kill herself rather than go to Pakistan, and her family would follow her and beat her to death wherever she went. Therefore, she says, she has no other option. "I will shoot anybody who tries to take this gun away from me. No one will make me live the life they want for me."

Police are called and they ping the cell phone and get a "lat/long." Because of the gun, a negotiator takes over the call from the crisis line.

Making it Challenging

If desired, you can make this exercise really interesting. The role player WILL be in a car somewhere outside your city. You will ping the cell-phone and try to locate her. A negotiator talks with her on the phone, while this is going on. Once she is located, you will be making a decision on whether the phone negotiator continues to speak with her, or if you wish to change to another mode of communication. You could use this exercise to train your SWAT officers on proper use of cover behind vehicles and the like, and even the horrifying dilemma of shoot-no/shoot if you have the role player, obviously a young girl, exit the car with the gun in her hand.

---

12 – Interview with Parents

The family denies all of Amira's claims. They claim that they condemn honor killing, and would never do such a thing. They admit they have been arranging a marriage for their daughter. This is part of their culture, and it is a matter of religious and cultural freedom. Her father quickly becomes angry with interviewers, and in addition, states he will not allow his daughter to communicate with them, because she is a good girl and is not allowed to speak with strange men. She is only allowed to speak with police with her father or brother present. They have contacted a lawyer, who maintains this is a matter of religious freedom and he has a court order to protect the child from police intrusion.

Amira, however, continues to adamantly assert that she is telling the truth. Unless the negotiator can offer her a way out, she will surely kill herself.

Training for Legal Issues in Culturally-Sensitive Cases

Another interesting challenge would be to use the services of a lawyer who has researched such cases in court. Admin can train on stalling tactics, coordination with their own legal advisor to keep the family/their lawyer out of the negotiation, while taking care to keep the agency as safe as possible from toxic litigation.

12 – Cultural Consult

There is, in larger municipal areas, enough potential for a case like this to occur that you should use this role play as an opportunity to research where you can find a consultant who is, whether Muslim or not, well versed in orthodox Islam and honor killing. This can be a valuable exercise if a) the consultant is supportive of HNT's goal to help the child b) defensive about what s/he sees as criticism of Muslim culture.

Effective Use of Cultural Consultation—and Effective Cultural Consultants

Honor killing is not exclusively a Muslim problem, but statistics show worldwide, well over 90% of honor murders are done within Muslim families. We have absolutely no intention of stigmatizing a culture or religion here—rather, officers must be prepared for various cultural rules that are dysfunctional and even destructive to its own members (name a culture for which this is not true!).

The information you are looking for from the consultant would be:

- What organizations support young women in these situations?
- Religious support for a young woman refusing to follow her parents' toxic wishes (this can help the young woman have a reason to live—this is not for argumentation with the parents),
- Information on how girls have survived and thrived after surviving situations like this. Because this is, in fact, a serious problem for some young women, it would be worthwhile to contact such potential consults beforehand so that if such a situation arises, you will know whom you can actually consult, and who will have agendas other than the well-being of such young women.

12 – Psychological Consult

The negotiator is talking to a young woman, who, although acculturated into America, does have to grapple with values alien to our culture. Beyond just trying to get her to talk about herself, getting her to talk about what she loves is probably a good idea. Ask her to explain about chemistry. There is both a hope and a risk here; the hope that if she talks about what she loves, she will increasingly desire to live and fight for her dream. The risk is that it may feel like salt in her wounds.

If she becomes, therefore, despairing because her parents are making her lose her chemistry, this is where you can talk about CPS involvement to protect her. Many states have CHINS statutes (Child in Need of Services) in which a court supports the child in her best needs), as well as "emancipation."

The previous cultural consult can help provide her, through you, with concrete information of successful girls in the same situation.

You want to be able to 'guarantee' she will not be forced back to her parents, so one of the negotiators should be making calls to ascertain what her rights are, based on similar court cases.

SCENARIO 12 – Checklist for After Action Review

The after action assessment/critique will depend on what was expressed and expected of the team going into the exercise. In other words, what was the desired training goal or outcome? Not just the outcome of the scenario, but what are the skills the director (team leader) is hoping to see exercised by the team, as these scenarios/situations develop?

Cultural issues important—how did team develop that?
- ❏ Did not meet goal
- ❏ Partially met goal
- ❏ Fully met goal

Did primary address suicidality issue head on?
- ❏ Did not meet goal
- ❏ Partially met goal
- ❏ Fully met goal

Contact expert?
- ❏ Did not meet goal
- ❏ Partially met goal
- ❏ Fully met goal

Demonstrate good listening skills
- ❏ Did not meet goal
- ❏ Partially met goal
- ❏ Fully met goal

SCENARIO 13

Frequent Caller, Borderline Personality

13 – Original Call

Possible suicide. Complainant, a mental health professional, states her patient called stating she has a gun and is going to shoot herself. The patient is at her own home, at (location) with her baby.

Officers respond, and using a cell phone, call inside. Brandi says, "I just want to shoot myself and die. Go away. You are making me nervous. Alicia is in my arms, and if you make me nervous, I might shoot her by mistake."

Officers request SWAT and HNT.

13 – Contact with Dispatch

Brandi is a chronic caller to the crisis line and to 9-1-1 services. Dispatch has been trying to work with the crisis line to more effectively handle these calls. She has made suicidal threats for a period of years, and people are quite burned out on her. She demands a lot of resources, costing the county a lot of money and taking officers and EMT off the road to respond to her calls. Until recently, the most she'd ever done was make hairline scratches on her wrists. Nonetheless, protocol demanded that police responded to her 9-1-1 calls.

A close friend, fed up after yet another crisis, decided to 'scare her straight.' He said, "If you were really serious about this suicide, you wouldn't be fooling around with those little scratches. You'd cut lengthwise from here (pointing to her elbow) to here (pointing to her wrists)." On her next attempt, Brandi made three cuts down to the bone, from elbow to wrists, losing 4 pints of blood. A roommate found her unconscious. She had almost died. Her arm is obscenely scarred. She cut too deeply for stitches to really close the wounds, and her forearm has three red, raised tracks, as if she has huge worms under the skin.

Brandi's three subsequent suicide attempts were more serious. She swallowed lye, jumped out of a third story window, and stabbed herself in the abdomen with a fish boning knife. It seems miraculous she's alive. She threw up the lye, causing some scarring in her throat, but no permanent damage. Some rhododendron bushes at the base of the house broke her fall out the window, and the knife somehow threaded its way past her internal organs, merely nicking her liver.

Brandi is, nonetheless, a sympathetic character to some. She is very attractive, and, when not suicidal or enraged, she has an angelic persona, a soft voice, emanating profound sadness and confusion. On one call to 9-1-1, she said, "I'm so sorry to be bothering you again. I hate myself so much. I know you people are tired of me. I just want to end it all, and I have no one to say goodbye to, but you."

13 – Interview with CPS Social Worker

The police have an interview with the CPS social worker, who speculates Brandi is overwhelmed by the responsibility of caring for her baby, despite her claims to want to reunite with her. She feels at fault whenever the baby cries, and this kid has colic, so he's crying all the time.

13 – Follow-up Interview with one EMT

You can, of course, change the profession to police, or the gender of the informant, whatever suits your available role-player.

She became fixated on one EMT, who made a few follow-up calls to check she was doing all right after the boning knife incident. They met for coffee. The EMT, new at her job, was trying to be concerned, but Brandi misinterpreted this. Brandi called the woman's husband at work to inform him that he didn't understand his wife's needs and there had to be some way, considering their kids, to allow them to continue the marriage while she could live out her bisexual nature. The EMT dealt with this as best she could in the circumstances, going immediately to her supervisor. The supervisor filed a report with the police, following their department policy. Now, however, in addition to everything else, her shift had to be 'flagged' so she wouldn't go out on calls to Brandi.

13 – Interview with Therapist

Tonight, Brandi has called her therapist, and told him she's fed up with being a burden. "I've read all the statistics on suicides and how women make more attempts that don't succeed because of the methods they use. You never believe I'm serious. I am. I hate myself. I got my dad's gun, oh God, will you tell him I'm sorry! I'm going to shoot myself in the head."

Child Protective Services has been involved with her, due to her incompetent caregiving of her baby, and after six months of foster care and supervised visits; they had just shifted to unsupervised visits a week ago.

Her therapist states Brandi has a borderline personality disorder, and notes traits of uncertainty about her sexuality, volatile relationships, rapid shifts from one mood to another, including rage, and idealization followed by a sense of betrayal regarding those close to her. "You will find her provocative and manipulative. She's not playing games, like a sociopath. She just reacts to whatever emotion she is feeling. I've found it best to notice when she is reactive and to shift the subject so she calms down. She will not 'listen to reason.' She only listens to what she feels in the moment."

Brandi will raise a history of sexual abuse. The therapist suggests the negotiator should commiserate in a matter-of-fact way, and state, "I wish I could have been there to stop it", and then, CHANGE THE SUBJECT. If she talks about her abuse, she will begin to relive it.

Effective Use of a Therapist for On-scene Consult

Feel free to use a psychotherapist as an on-scene consult, if you wish to include him or her in the exercise. What would be a valuable training exercise here would be to recruit a therapist familiar with borderline personality and give them the above schema. It would be a worthwhile aspect of HNT training to educate the therapist/consultant on what YOU need from them while having them on scene. (This replaces the usual psych consult that we have in most chapters).

---

13 – How This Scenario Should Play Out For Maximum Education On Borderline Personality

Brandi is going to run through two negotiators. With the first, the negotiator will make headway. Brandi will be very sweet—a sympathetic character. The negotiator will think this will soon resolve, viewing Brandi as just an uncertain young woman, who needs support and encouragement. Brandi, after idealizing the negotiator, and telling him/her how wonderful he or she is, will suddenly decide she is being talked down to and become utterly enraged. She will begin to make threats to kill herself and her baby if she has to talk to the negotiator anymore. The negotiator should be put in a place of thinking, "What the hell just happened? Everything was going so well." Brandi will be in hysterical, screaming rage.

Eventually, a second negotiator should take over.

If the negotiation team gets stubborn and refuses to change over, Brandi should continue to escalate, and if the team doesn't get the message, she should kill herself (and even her baby, if the team leader decides such a harsh lesson is necessary).

Once a change-over is accomplished, and some rapport is established, Brandi will demand to talk to the EMT whom she is infatuated with. She will be stuck on this for quite some time. It will be the task of the negotiator to shift her to focusing on the future, get her to IMAGINE her child happy with her. She will be sensitive to being manipulated, and even more sensitive to someone trying to make her feel good by giving her empty put-ups.

Transition from One Negotiator to Another

This is a good scenario to practice transitioning from one negotiator to another. With an individual with borderline personality, the rapport developed is very superficial and fleeting on the part of the subject, anyway, so it's not going to be permanent with ANY negotiator you place as primary. Take it as an opportunity to practice doing transitions, and switch out more often than you normally do.

SCENARIO 13 – Checklist for After Action Review

The after action assessment/critique will depend on what was expressed and expected of the team going into the exercise. In other words, what was the desired training goal or outcome? Not just the outcome of the scenario, but what are the skills the director (team leader) is hoping to see exercised by the team, as these scenarios/situations develop?

Develop floor plan
- ❏ Did not meet goal
- ❏ Partially met goal
- ❏ Fully met goal

Demonstrate good listening skills
- ❏ Did not meet goal
- ❏ Partially met goal
- ❏ Fully met goal

Develop transition plan to switch out negotiators
- ❏ Did not meet goal
- ❏ Partially met goal
- ❏ Fully met goal

Transition successfully
- ❏ Did not meet goal
- ❏ Partially met goal
- ❏ Fully met goal

Consider psych consult on this one
- ❏ Did not meet goal
- ❏ Partially met goal
- ❏ Fully met goal

SCENARIO 14

School Phobia, Obsessive-Compulsive Disorder in Teen

14 – Original Call

Possible suicide attempt. Teenage son, barricaded in upstairs bedroom with a knife, threatening to kill himself. Officers arrive, are met by the parents outside.

14 – Interview with Parents

One of the parents should be hyper-emotional. The hyper-emotional parent will be criticizing the other for not taking the problem seriously enough. The interviewer(s) will first practice de-escalation skills; perhaps you will have to separate them. There should be a lot of interruptions between the parents as you try to get the information.

Ari refused to go to school this morning. His father fed up with asking and nagging, tried to physically pull him out of bed and carry him downstairs. Ari just went dead-weight, and the father slipped, they both fell, and when dad hit the floor, he threw his back out. Dad lost it and for the first time in family memory, cursed his son. Ari grabbed a knife from the kitchen, ran upstairs to his parent's room, and is currently sitting on his parents' bed, yelling out that he will cut his throat and his father can sleep the rest of eternity in the blood.

After hopelessly trying to get him to give up the knife, including begging, offering concessions, yelling, and anything else two desperate parents might try, they called 9-1-1.

14 –Background Information

This is the information that the role player will have—and what Intel will acquire if and only if they succeed in an effective interview with the family.

Ari is the third son of a modern Orthodox Jewish family. What this means is they keep fairly strict rituals regarding diet and expected ethical behavior, yet also accept modern life. Ari's mom works outside the home, and they are familiar with and accepting of American culture.

As is typical of Orthodox Jewish families, school and learning is a huge priority. Ari's father is a graduate of MIT and his mother from Brandeis University with a degree in evolutionary psychology. Ari's two old brothers are National Merit Scholars, one going to Princeton and the other to Caltech.

Ari, too, is quite bright, but has always hated school. He has a tendency to obsess on things, and believes he must do everything perfect or he is a complete failure. For example, he got a score of 2387 (out of 2400) on his SAT, and he was so upset he started screaming at his mother when she praised him. He was sitting on the couch at the time and slammed the heels of his shoes down on the coffee table so hard the glass shattered, and he needed 47 stitches on his calf muscle.

Ari has always been an obedient kid, but ever since 4th grade, he would frequently refuse to go to school and his father would have to manhandle him into the car and take him there. This made him late to work, his boss was unsympathetic, and this stressed the whole family.

Things were better in junior high and high school. He had a girlfriend and they have been inseparable. She's a very stable young lady, and usually can joke with him about his obsessive traits. However, Ari's been in a tailspin since his 'failure' on the SAT. He's stopped talking with her.

14 – Notes for the Role Player

Ari's been in therapy for many years. He is familiar with active listening and reframing. He is somewhat arrogant, and he believes he is smarter than most of the people around (that's probably true). This is going to make things difficult for the negotiator, because Ari will know things about communication techniques better than you. In addition, because of his obsessive nature, he will nit-pick everything the negotiator says. He will be patronizing, and a step ahead.

A difficult role-play – ethnic, cultural and philosophical issues

There is no doubt this will be a difficult role to play. You will need someone who is well read. They do not have to be a youth, but they have to be able to play young. This role-play, of course, does NOT have to play Orthodox Jewish. It will do just as well if the role player is familiar with another culture. Just rewrite the script anyway you like, the family could be Chinese American, with a 'tiger mom,' obsessed with education, or a middle class African-American family—whatever the role players can play well. The 'trap' for the negotiator will be he or she must not try to 'prove' he or she understands this youth's world.

---

14 – The Scene: Face-to-Face or On the Phone?

The team leader can organize this exercise in a variety of ways.

1. The entire exercise could be on the phone. The negotiator is informed that there is a phone in the room or that Ari has a cell phone—or SWAT can exercise getting a phone to Ari, using anything from a throw-phone through the window to a robot.

2. The officer/negotiator approaches the room. He sees Ari sitting on a bed, with the knife to his throat. Ari threatens to kill himself if the negotiator comes closer. The negotiator withdraws immediately, and they use electronic means of communication.

3. The officer/negotiator attempts to speak with Ari either in line of sight, or around a corner. In this case, Ari must NOT make any overtly threatening gestures to the officer, but he should, at times, wave the knife around as he talks. Even though the officer warns him about this, he'll forget and do it again. Ari will state the following right at the beginning: "I know you are thinking of Tazing me to get this knife away. But I've been watching videos on YouTube showing the paralysis of the Taser is only inside the probes. Look it up! Washington State Criminal Justice Training Commission has all their recruits get Tased for thirty seconds and they all have to try to shoot Simunitions. Almost everyone can do it. I won't be able to move my body, but I will be able to stab myself in the throat." Depending on the goals of the team leader, a negotiation *could* continue face-to-face, or at the right moment, the officer(s) could withdraw and communicate by phone.

Don't push the Issue!

The third option could be an interesting training exercise. There have been a number of incidents where officers attempt to assist a suicidal individual, who tells them to keep back. Sometimes they are frightened and other times they are defiant. The officer(s) sometimes push the issue, moving forward rather than back, and when the suicidal individual makes what appears to be (or actually is) a threatening gesture, the latter is shot, even killed. This exercise can be used to drive home the necessity of tactical withdrawal. The team-leader can set things up in such a way that, unless there is a reason for a hard lesson to be learned, another member of the team can, when necessary, yell, "Pull back! We'll talk to him on the phone!"

---

14 – Interviews with the Girlfriend and the Brothers

Among other things, use the interview to get information on their culture.

The girlfriend should be shy and hard to interview. Even if not Orthodox Jewish, we want someone from an insular culture, who is hesitant about talking about what is 'inside.'

If possible, get the brothers on the phone. One of them, at least, should be patronizing and obnoxious, pushing the interviewer's buttons with intellectual arrogance.

14 – What the Role Player will Reveal as the Interview Progresses – More Instructions for the Role Player

As the exercise unfolds, it will become increasingly clear this is not just a kid with an attitude. The level of his OCD is pathological; he is precise and nit-picky about everything.

- Initially, you will only hear how much he hates school. The automatic assumption will be he is being bullied. If the negotiator pushes this, Ari will get angrier. He is not bullied at school. In fact, other kids like him. He's always been the kind of kid who hides his distress, as did the family. They never let the school know about his phobia.
- Ari's obsessive traits will become more and more prominent.
- Only after rapport is established will Ari reveal that school is not just unpleasant for him, it is a horrifying phobia that completely takes him over. He has a pervasive, unexplainable sense of terror at the thought of going to school. With his girlfriend at his side, this was manageable, but since they became estranged, he feels isolated and alone.

Another important point, about four months ago, he agreed to take Luvox, an SSRI medication similar to Prozac.

Medication Consult

Anytime the person mentions taking medications, it is a good idea to get a medical consult on the effects of the medications: why they are used; what possible side-effects might occur; what will happen if they run out of the medications.

In this case, a good child psychiatrist or other expert on the effects of psychiatric meds on kids would discuss the occasional side-effects of anti-depressant SSRI's. They can have paradoxical, agitating effects on teens. It is possible good information regarding medications may be useful to discuss with Ari. This should be up to your team to figure out, although if they don't, the psych consult can bring this up.

---

14 – Psychological Consult and Medical Consult

INITIAL CONSULT: OCD

This kid is a therapy veteran. He is familiar with paraphrasing and active listening, so you will have to be sparing when you use it. Rather, you try to establish a dialogue. Certainly try to have him come out, but be prepared for Ari to reject this and expect a long conversation, building rapport simply through dialogue.

As for communication, don't pretend his nit-picking doesn't exist. Approach it with good humor, but don't tease him. He will take jokes as an assault. These obsessions and detail orientation are deadly serious to him. This is the kind of person who will become enraged if an item on his desk is a ¼ inch out of place.

<u>Note to the consultant</u>, If the negotiator has been assuming that Ari is being bullied, and they are stuck at an impasse, suggest that something else might be going on, which will lead you to talk about obsessive-compulsive behaviors. The negotiator should empathize how difficult it must be to have to be so concerned with details.

He will regard this incident as a failure. Without any patronization, without any attempt to 'build up his self-esteem' (which he'll regard with contempt), you will have to figure out with him a reason to surrender. It will have to be framed as a problem-solving exercise that, if the meds have been disrupting his abilities, they must be changed, if going to school in it's present form is impossible, how will he get educated, etc.

SECOND LEVEL CONSULT: SCHOOL PHOBIA

Once Ari reveals his school phobia, the consultant should assist the negotiator in understanding this is far more than dislike of school. For Ari, school fills him with irrational emotions, possibly including rage and terror. Don't try to establish rapport by telling how you didn't like school (or some other activity) yourself. This is NOT dislike. It is a serious psychological disturbance. All you can do is listen and express sympathy, in regards to this.

THIRD LEVEL CONSULT: THE SURRENDER

The negotiator's task is to make a VERY detailed surrender plan with him, and collaborate on the details. Be meticulous, but clear. You should both announce each step together, going over them in a checklist fashion. (And note that Ari may give you suggestions on how to 'improve' your plan. Don't get offended or patronize him—if it's a good idea, accept it. If it's not a good idea, calmly reject it, succinctly explain why and direct what you will be doing instead).

SCENARIO 14 – Checklist for After Action Review

The after action assessment/critique will depend on what was expressed and expected of the team going into the exercise. In other words, what was the desired training goal or outcome? Not just the outcome of the scenario, but what are the skills the director (team leader) is hoping to see exercised by the team, as these scenarios/situations develop?

Floor plan developed
- ❏ Did not meet goal
- ❏ Partially met goal
- ❏ Fully met goal

Demonstrate good listening skills
- ❏ Did not meet goal
- ❏ Partially met goal
- ❏ Fully met goal

Follow up on the medications subject is taking
- ❏ Did not meet goal
- ❏ Partially met goal
- ❏ Fully met goal

Call in/request medical consult
- ❏ Did not meet goal
- ❏ Partially met goal
- ❏ Fully met goal

Did negotiator work out a satisfactory surrender plan?
- ❏ Did not meet goal
- ❏ Partially met goal
- ❏ Fully met goal

SCENARIO 15

Divorce, Visitation Conflict, Histrionic Personality in Mother vs. Trapped Desperation/Depression in Father

> **Double Scenario**
> This can be played at the same time as two scenarios, particularly if you have a large team to train. This way, there will be fewer negotiators just standing around watching. If you have officers who are waiting to become negotiators, and you want to give them some experience practicing with the team, this would be a good exercise to use.

15 – Original Call
See the woman about custodial interference. Estranged husband has left with the children in a vehicle (provide description, etc.)

Cassandra, a mother of four-year-old twins calls, saying her estranged ex-husband, whom she refers to as Arnie, has kidnapped the children during a visitation. She says that he has a history of domestic violence against her, and manipulation of the children. The courts awarded her primary custody and he has been allowed unsupervised visitation two weekends a month.

15 – Directions for the Role Player of Cassandra and Training Goals for Negotiator
Mother will be distraught, accusatory and will bring in all sorts of extraneous information. She will talk about her conflicts with the father, and react to your questions defensively, as if you are accusing her of something. For example, the negotiator will certainly try get information on what kind of car the father is driving, if he made any threats, whether he has ever harmed or threatened to harm the kids. After fifteen minutes, you will know little more than the make/model of the car. You will have heard a LOT about the conflicts between Cassandra and Arnie, the father. You will not know what the father's intentions are. This is so difficult you contact a psychological consult.

15 – Psychological Consultation Regarding Mother
Your psych consult is present and listens to the contact with the mother. S/he states the mother displays traits known as "histrionic personality;" in the vernacular, often called a "drama queen." Whatever she feels in the moment, she needs the world to know about—and respond in a way that she finds rewarding. Such individuals 'talk in headlines'—it is very difficult to get them to talk specifically. For example, you ask, "What was your dad like?" And they reply, "Oh wow, he was, I don't know, a fuckin' explosion, I mean impact! Walk in a room and wow!

Furthermore, they get 'energy' from the drama; they often forget the real crisis, as they become preoccupied with their own feelings. There are several tactics that might help with this person. You will have to try each of them, in turn:

1. If you can set up a communication style where you are a warm paternal or maternal figure, such people can sometimes desire to please you more than create drama.

2. Paraphrase in a way that you get increasingly specific, where she has to fill in the blank: For example:
   - You are really desperate. You are really desperate because you are afraid you husband is going to . . .
   - You are telling me that you are really desperate because you are afraid your husband is going to do something terrible . . . to the kids.
   - You don't know what he's going to do. You are telling me he's done bad things in the past. Tell me what bad things has he done to the kids in the past.
   - ETC.

3. Speak very firmly (not loudly or stridently), telling her how important it is that you get detailed information.

If you try to guilt-trip her, criticize her or express frustration, she will respond with more drama.

15 – Contact with Subject
<u>Second part of this exercise: Patrol has spotted the father's car, and has made the stop, and has requested HNT and SWAT, based on the following information.</u>

Father's car is spotted and police follow. When father sees police car, he accelerates to escape, but when police put on flashers, he pulls into a Costco parking lot. It is after hours, and the lot is empty. When police approach the vehicle, father puts gun to own head, and waves police away. When one officer attempts to talk to him, he shakes his head, and waves the gun towards one of the children. Police establish a perimeter, and the negotiation team is called. They note the father does not appear mad; his facial expression is glum and hopeless.

TECH ADDITIONS:
1. Father will talk through cell phone.
2. In background, there should be a continuous loop of loud crying kids.
3. It would be better if you use lifelike child figures. This will allow the role player to be threatening, without frightening real kids, and will also allow the possibility of a violent outcome to the scenario.

15 – Interview with Former Employer
Previous employer is contacted. He states, "The guy was a good worker. I knew he smoked marijuana, but 'a lot of my guys do.'" He worked in a shipyard, doing decking on high-end yachts. The father was terminated after he heard he was being charged with domestic violence. "I don't know any details. I just don't like guys around who hit women."

15 – Info for Role-Player

Father is going to be leaden. He sees no hope in negotiating. He will not be aggressive towards the children; rather, he'll be patient and gentle with the kids (you will hear him, unsuccessfully, trying to calm the kids down, but he won't get mad at them). He didn't get into a high-speed chase—he slowly turned into Costco. Nonetheless, he will say his intention is to shoot self and kids. This is going to be a slow negotiation process, with a lot of "I don't know", "what's the point," "No one cares," No one listens to me," "So that's the way you see it?" Father will laugh cynically at things.

He is going to give very little. He makes no overt movement to threaten kids, unless this is a joint SWAT exercise, and any movement by the SWAT team will be countered by his pointing the gun towards the children – finger not indexed. If the goal is to train SWAT sniper member, however, it should be set up that an escalation is 'programmed' into his response so that the sniper can properly aim and simulate taking him out (BUT do not do this until most of the rest of this exercise is concluded—there's still a lot of practice to be done!)

15 – Further direction for Role-Player

Tone of voice should be flat and hopeless. However, when officer calls you Arnie, you should blow up. "Fuck you! My name is Ernie. SHE calls me Arnie, the fucking bitch! It's not my fucking name!" Cut the phone. If the officer makes the mistake again, later in negotiation, escalate dangerously. Were the negotiator to make the mistake three times, the role-player should start howling and shoot self and kids.

15 – #2 – Further Info

Secondary negotiation/crisis stabilization training can be done with mom. She will continue, face-to-face, to be hysterical with a second negotiator. She will also be demanding, accusatory ("You don't care about my kids") and distraught. She will threaten suicide if the children are killed, and on the other hand, offer to kill herself if that will lead "Arnie" to let the kids go. She will stabilize somewhat with one of the strategies suggested by your consultant, but you must use them all to find what works.

15 – Contact with Ernie's Mother

Ernie's mom is contacted. Another negotiator can do an interview with her. She brings several documents. (She can read the information below). The officer should take notes and carry this to the team.

1. First is a psych evaluation, in which mother is diagnosed as histrionic personality. The evaluator cites the mother as having engaged in "abusive use of conflict" to alienate the children from the father, and furthermore, states she is an incompetent mother, who is easily overwhelmed. The psychologist states that the children are clearly stressed in the mother's presence. He writes that Ernie is a passive guy, not very talkative, whom the children love. He notes dad does not get down on the floor and play with the boys, and reads to them in a monotone. He states that the children are less stressed with dad, but they "don't do very much." They sometimes simply lean against him, while he sits quietly with his arms around them.

The psychologist ends his report with a small personal "opinion essay," in which he notes that children are resilient, and that, in some ways, a passive inexpressive parent is, in his opinion, just as bad as an aggressive, untrustworthy, manipulative one. He states he sees no problems with the father, except he doesn't have a 'playful personality.' He concludes that there is a special bond between mothers and children, even when the mother is incompetent or psychologically 'less than optimum,' and this should be broken only in the most serious of circumstances.

2. The judge writes an opinion essentially accepting what the psychologist says, and awards primary custody to the mother.

3. The next is a police report. It describes a visitation 'hand-off' where mom confronted dad, questioning his sexual competence in front of the children. He tried to get the kids in the car, and she began repeatedly poking him in the forehead with an index finger. He asked her to stop several times, and she replied he should appreciate being poked, because that's about all he was ever able to do to her. She said she and her new boyfriend liked to lie in bed after sex and laugh about 'Arnie's' lack of endowment and inability to satisfy her. He pleaded with her to stop talking like that in front of the children. When she poked him again (officer noted a red spot between his eyes, with small scratches), he shoved her away. She fell over, and from the ground, whipped out a cell phone and called 9-1-1. Father was arrested, and charged with domestic violence. Charges were later dropped.

4. A final document is a follow-up hearing, in which the judge notes the 'set-up' in the police report. Mother denies the actions in the police report and states the officers, being men, sided with 'Arnie.' In her account, she describes 'Arnie' sneering at her, and calling her an incompetent mother, and when she pleaded with him to stop for the sake of the children, he shoved her to the ground. The judge writes her account is not believable, but states it "does not rise to the level in which a change in the parenting plan should be considered." Furthermore, the judge decrees that, just to err on the side of caution, "even though there is no evidence of any domestic violence," <u>Ernie is required to undertake a domestic violence evaluation at his own expense</u>. This last document is dated one week previous to the current incident.

The Story Changes: Shifting Gears in the Middle of a Negotiation

What tack should the negotiator take to get Ernie to surrender and allow the kids to be safe? Should you continue with the same negotiator? One possible option would be for the first negotiator to state: "Ernie, we've got some information from your mom. This changes things." Perhaps that negotiator will continue, or perhaps it would be a good time to have a new negotiator on the phone, to 'start afresh.'

Depending on the decision of the director, based on preferred training needs, one could program this to:

1. A surrender of father and children
2. A surrender of children, followed by a request by the father to "Please take them away from here," and then a suicide.
3. An escalation: a) in the car b) changing his mind at the point of surrender c) suicide by cop necessitating SWAT to neutralize the threat he presents.

SCENARIO 15 – Checklist for After Action Review

The after action assessment/critique will depend on what was expressed and expected of the team going into the exercise. In other words, what was the desired training goal or outcome? Not just the outcome of the scenario, but what are the skills the director (team leader) is hoping to see exercised by the team, as these scenarios/situations develop?

Tactical plan developed
- ❏ Did not meet goal
- ❏ Partially met goal
- ❏ Fully met goal

Demonstrate good listening skills
- ❏ Did not meet goal
- ❏ Partially met goal
- ❏ Fully met goal

Appropriately calmed the mother
- ❏ Did not meet goal
- ❏ Partially met goal
- ❏ Fully met goal

Requested/discussed using psych consult
- ❏ Did not meet goal
- ❏ Partially met goal
- ❏ Fully met goal

Intel worked to locate/contact key players
- ❏ Did not meet goal
- ❏ Partially met goal
- ❏ Fully met goal

SCENARIO 16

Hostage Taking in the Commission of a Crime with Hysterical Victims and Volatile Hostage Takers

16 – On-View Incident

Call to 9-1-1, simultaneous to patrol officers being flagged down by a witness, who reported having witnessed an armed robbery at a convenience store. A man inside the store was brutally assaulted, and a knife was seen. The on-view officers contained the scene, have suspects and hostages inside, and have called for HNT and SWAT.

16 – The Incident

Carmine and D'Andre are on a cough syrup high. They walked into a small market to buy some snacks. They stacked up about $25 worth of various junk food packages, only then realizing that neither remembered their wallet. It is intellectually too large a task to either put the stuff back on the shelves or simply leave, so D'Andre flicks open his pocketknife, and says, "Put the stuff in a bag, bitch." Among the shoppers is a retired police officer, aged 67, who is working at the store as security. He attempts to intervene, pulling an ASP baton and yelling at the miscreants to "drop the knife and hit the floor."

Carmine is stupid, he is stoned, and he is also immense. He lumbers forward and the retired officer hits him in the head with the baton. It's too high up on the skull and Carmine simply bear-hugs the man, picks him up and drops all 420 pounds on top of him, breaking three ribs. Enraged at the pain of the head strike, Carmine punches the retired officer multiple times in the face, breaking the orbital bones around both eye sockets.

One of the shoppers has called police on her cell phone, and another managed to run out as Carmine continued his brutal assault. The last thing he sees is Carmine heaving himself up off the unconscious man. The witness flags down police, and gives a description of the incident.

16 – The Setting

Aside from the unconscious security guard, there are three hostages. D'Andre will start out on the phone, although Carmine may, on occasion, rip it out of his hands to yell obscenities and threats.

The hostages will be hysterical. They should be yelling in the background, either crying for help, or yelling at the hostage takers. This will stress the hostage takers.

The hostage takers will be mild-to-moderately stoned, more stupid and panicked than psychotic or delirious.

The hostage takers are not going to come up with very rational demands. Not to say that they won't come up with something, however, outlandish.

16 – Interview with Mother

Carmine's mother is on scene. She lives only a few blocks away and had actually been walking down the street trying to follow the 'boys' as they lurched down the street in their El Camino in second gear. She will be an interesting interview. She will be salty, irreverent, and a little funny.

According to her and other relatives, Carmine loves his mother. D'Andre, an abandoned child whom she took in, is "like a stray puppy, if puppies ever were the size of baby elephants." Of the two of them, she says, "What can I tell you? They don't mean no harm. Think of the Three Stooges on drugs with weapons. That's my boys."

She describes the early part of the evening in the following manner: Carmine and D'Andre first gorged on instant microwave curry, the only thing they could find in the house. They each drank three large-size bottles of cough syrup, and after one-half hour of cough syrup mixed with instant curry burps, they seemed to be shifting between blurred vision and hallucinations. Their judgment is just a little bit impaired, not that it was very good before their 'discount delirium.'

After a number of bumbling hours, Carmine broke D'Andre's stereo, and they got in a mutually ineffectual fistfight. They left the bathroom in a state so disgusting mom asks if the police could designate it a Superfund site. Eventually, the two guys decided to go for a ride. D'Andre stripped the gears of the El Camino, while still in the driveway, and put two new creases in the passenger side door. They lurched down the street in second gear. That's when mom walked out of the house after them

16 – Possible Training on TPI

One possible avenue of training is to use the mother in controlled negotiation. As the reader is well aware, this is, almost always NOT a good idea, but there have been cases in which the relative, closely monitored and prepped, is used in this manner. Most teams NEVER allow such collateral contact—therefore, do not abandon your protocol. Only use this segment if it is part of the protocol of your team. The idea here would be to use it as a practice, in case it is ever deemed the best idea.

This is a good exercise for a team leader to test the decision-making skills and assessment abilities of the team. This can be set up so not only does the mom make the offer, but Carmine and D'Andre also make the same demand. As in: "MOM! MOM! Are you out there, mom? I wanna talk to my mom!!!!!"

What does the team do? Do they agree without much thought or investigation? If so, bring mom on.... and then, whoops, she lights up Carmine and D'Andre and bad things happen.

However, if the team explores as an option, it might allow them to practice for a potential TPI. Do they thoroughly interview the mother, to determine if she is stable and can be controlled? Do they have equipment with a 'kill switch' on her mic, if necessary? Or, maybe the team wishes to practice the method of having the mother make a recorded statement to be played to Carmine and D'Andre, something that could be played in a straightforward manner, or the role player could make it really challenging. All of these are valuable training options.

For the sake of TPI practice:

- Do not be casual about this. One should go through the entire preparation of the subject, coaching, rehearsal, and putting her on the phone.
- Let us imagine, on the other hand, that SWAT is fully deployed and ready to go. The relative could be used, where she suddenly yells a warning, or otherwise sets off the hostage takers. SWAT will not be cued as to this. The hostage takers will suddenly go berserk, and all things done properly, SWAT should immediately enter to neutralize them.

On the Use of TPI

The writers are well aware how badly a TPI call can go, and how rare that this is a viable option. However, it is very common that the public believes it is a good idea, and it frequently comes up in court. Family members and their attorneys assert that had they been allowed on the phone, the subject would have absolutely surrendered. One good training exercises for the team is to consider and prepare for TPI in good faith, so that your agency can assert honestly in court that you have the tools if/when it is ever a possibility—and can then assert that through that preparation, it was clearly established that it was NOT a good idea in this case.

The team can also try this and film it, to prepare for a future court case, showing how quickly such an incident can get out of control. With the family member on the phone, yelling, perhaps, at the hostage-takers and amping them up, this could prove a useful illustration were the question is ever to be raised in a lawsuit why the team didn't use family members as TPI. It also would be a good lead-in for SWAT to get practice on entry/taking out the hostage takers and rescuing the hostages.

16 – Psychological Consult

Whenever negotiating with intoxicated subjects, time is of the essence—MORE time. As the drugs are purged from the system, the individual often becomes more rational: in other cases, they get tired. One avenue of negotiation that opens up is the fact that the negotiator can become the agent of relief. If the hostage taker complies, they have a chance of sleep, food or an end to stress.

Crucial will be calming and reassuring tactics, because, in their panic, with the hostages FREQUENTLY losing it, the hostage takers may be moved to beat someone into submission or cut someone's throat just for a little peace and quiet.

Therefore the negotiator will be pressured to calm them down, and with the team, may brainstorm *with them* ways to calm down the hostages as well. One idea will be to suggest to the hostage takers that with the hostages out, they can have peace and quiet.

These guys are not bright, but they surely have some street cunning. The negotiator should, of course, be trying to get various hostages out, first and foremost the injured security guard.

1. The negotiator may say, "You have the power here. And we'll definitely figure out a way to work this thing out. But if the guard dies, everything changes. Anyway, you didn't intend for it to happen, so if you just move him to the doorway, we can take him away, and calm things down for all of us.

2. If they offer to release another hostage, of course accept them.

3. Return, however, to the injured guard. With these guys, making a deal for pizzas or other food is likely to be the way to go.

4. I would suggest keeping them bonded, rather than a divide-and-conquer strategy. If these two stupid, impulse ridden guys get arguing, one of them may hurt a hostage to take control over from the other. Rather, emphasize how they are brothers, and they'll get out of this together. They've got each other's back, and they'll be able to work this out with the judge.

SCENARIO 16 – Checklist for After Action Review

The after action assessment/critique will depend on what was expressed and expected of the team going into the exercise. In other words, what was the desired training goal or outcome? Not just the outcome of the scenario, but what are the skills the director (team leader) is hoping to see exercised by the team, as these scenarios/situations develop?

Floor plan developed? From whom did you get the information?
- ❏ Did not meet goal
- ❏ Partially met goal
- ❏ Fully met goal

Demonstrate good listening skills
- ❏ Did not meet goal
- ❏ Partially met goal
- ❏ Fully met goal

Do negotiators change tactics because a law enforcement officer is involved?
- ❏ Did not meet goal
- ❏ Partially met goal
- ❏ Fully met goal

Discussion/decision regarding use of TPI?
- ❏ Did not meet goal
- ❏ Partially met goal
- ❏ Fully met goal

Do negotiators successfully bid for release of hostages?
- ❏ Did not meet goal
- ❏ Partially met goal
- ❏ Fully met goal

SCENARIO 17

Hostage Taking on Prison Site

17 – Alert at the Prison

Hostage taking in the education office, situation in lockdown. Subject barricaded with 3 hostages. Requesting immediate SWAT and HNT response.

17 – The Incident

This information would be a combination of information known to SWAT, and a report to SWAT by a correctional officer or case manager.

Inmate Cliff Powell went into an office and found his teacher and two support staff personnel alone. He slammed the door, locked and barricaded it, and pulled a blade.

There is only a single fence beyond this office, and the work camp is in a wilderness area, about ten miles from any town or residential area. There is only a single road, and the forest around the camp is a wetlands area, very soggy, and full of downed trees and brush. No one has successfully escaped from this work-camp. Everyone gets bogged down in the wetlands. At any rate, there are few escape attempts. The inmates are almost all short-timers or those with minor felonies who, if they do their time, will soon be released.

It is unknown if Cliff intended to try to escape. He did open the window on the second story nearest to the fence, and this is how he was spotted. Upon the correctional officer's yell, he pulled back into the room.

He has, therefore, three hostages, and no exit. His first move was to pull the phone out of the wall-jack, so communication is initially difficult.

Is this is an escape attempt, a sexual assault attempt, both or something else?

17 – Background – Institutional Record Review

Cliff Powell has nine months left on eight-year sentence for felonious assault. Therefore, it is very odd he'd do something like this so close to release.

He is twenty-eight years old. He spent considerable time in detention as an adolescent, and according to his file, was diagnosed with ADHD and other unnamed impulse control disorders.

His current conviction was the result of a fight. Cliff had been taking Ecstasy on a daily basis, and became physiologically insensitive to the drug. He thought he was cheated, therefore, when the two hits he took didn't get him high. He went into the bar's restroom—the dealers 'office'—and jumped him from behind, ramming his head onto the lip of a toilet bowl, fracturing his skull.

In detention, Cliff has not gotten into serious trouble. On two occasions, he got into altercations with other inmates. On one, he assumed the other inmate was not going to eat his desert and he just took it, receiving a beating for the trespass. On the other, an inmate objected to his standing next to his bunk—violating rules of personal space and territory. Cliff won this fight, but did a period of time in administrative segregation.

He has been in a minimum-security work camp for approximately one year, taking classes to get his GED.

17 – Further Record Review
Review of his records shows he has an adolescent history of sexual offences. He and two friends, imitating a nasty fad from Japan called 'sharking,' would videotape each other, as one of them would walk up to a woman and either rip her blouse open, or yank her skirt down, and then run away. They posted these on the Internet, which is how they were caught.

A trustee inmate, who was in the same GED class notes Cliff occasionally made slightly 'flirtatious' jokes. The teacher set limits pretty well, to which Cliff would respond, "just kidding," or "I didn't say nothing."

17 – Interview with Case Manager
Cliff's case manager notes he was really anxious about "getting back in the world. He'd say, 'I don't know nothing, don't know how to do nothing.'"

The case manager also notes that Cliff was raped in his initial incarceration, and was the 'wife'—sex slave—of one of the dominant inmates of that penitentiary. He states Cliff seems to be unsure about his masculinity. "He doesn't open up much, but there was one meeting when he asked, 'Can you be turned into a gay? I mean, you start out liking girls, but something happens and then you are gay? I mean, how would you know? You don't have no way to test things out. And the admin here, they won't even let you have skin mags. So how do you know?"

17 – Directions for the Role Player
Cliff is going to be somewhat goofy—like a class clown. He will mess around, crack jokes, and it will be hard to focus him. A negotiator may be tempted to just tell him to open the damn door and let the ladies out. "You did something stupid, you'll get some time tacked on, but it's no big deal."

Cliff won't bite. In fact, he won't even engage with this.

He will threaten to cut the women just to warn the negotiator not to send in a SWAT team.

During the initial contact, if the negotiator is male, and is warm, soft-spoken, or 'supportive,' Cliff is going to be extremely hostile, accusing the negotiator of being a 'fag.' He will become increasingly hostile about this.

17 – Psychological Consult

The consultant suggests they don't know his motive, and the best way to find out is to keep listening, paraphrasing, and subtly keep trying to direct the conversation so he talks about himself.

The initial task of the negotiator here is to be patient. The negotiator will be thinking, "What's the point of all this. He's just messing around."

The negotiator has to hang in there, and just keep him talking.

The consultant is concerned this may possibly be for the purpose of a sexual assault so Cliff can prove to himself he's still a 'man' and not 'a gay.' The danger they face is, of course, they will be trying to negotiate the hostages out, which is often a one-by-one process. However, Cliff may draw this out, in order to make the negotiator(s) think they are making progress, and when he has one left—given his previous flirtation, probably the teacher—he very possibly will sexually assault her.

Caution ONE: If Cliff reveals his fears about being homosexual (which he might, although denying it, actually be) and the negotiator is too quick to reassure him, this reassurance will sound hollow and he will escalate. Therefore, continue to be low-key, rather than overly reassuring.

Caution TWO: Given Cliff's fears of being homosexual, and the fact he is resistive to the idea is not necessarily evidence he is not gay, he will be hair-trigger suspicious of other males. If the negotiator is too warm and reassuring, Cliff may either accuse him of being homosexual, or escalate, believing himself to being seduced. If this has resulted in an absolute impasse, consider shifting to a second negotiator. The best way to avoid this is for the interviewer to be a little formal, distant and matter-of-fact.

The negotiator should not reassure Cliff that it's "OK to be gay!" It's not OK to him. Rather, be noncommittal in tone, and agree when he says he's not gay. If he alludes to the rape 'making him gay,' you can respond that, just because someone does something to you doesn't mean it 'makes' you anything. If he is resistive, you can reduce it to an absurdity such as the following: 'Dude, if somehow a twenty-foot alligator jumped on you, it doesn't mean you like alligators.'

17 – Exercise Outcome

As time passes, you will be able to negotiate out one or two of the hostages through the usual, exchange of food or the like. In either event, the negotiator will be able to draw out, eventually, that Cliff IS afraid about his manhood. If the negotiator is calm, and doesn't get 'hooked' in over-reassuring him, he may eventually surrender.

On the other hand, if you wish SWAT to get their training in as well, Cliff will get more and more sexually suggestive in his talk and begin signaling a rape only takes a few minutes: "I mean, how long does it take a real man to get his nuts off, when he's not been emasculated by those feminists who tell him he has to think of their pleasure first?" As soon as the negotiator believes the scene is getting beyond his or her control, you should greenlight Tactical.

SCENARIO 17 – Checklist for After Action Review

The after action assessment/critique will depend on what was expressed and expected of the team going into the exercise. In other words, what was the desired training goal or outcome? Not just the outcome of the scenario, but what are the skills the director (team leader) is hoping to see exercised by the team, as these scenarios/situations develop?

Floor plan developed
- ❏ Did not meet goal
- ❏ Partially met goal
- ❏ Fully met goal

Demonstrate good listening skills
- ❏ Did not meet goal
- ❏ Partially met goal
- ❏ Fully met goal

Demonstrate EXTREME patience is key
- ❏ Did not meet goal
- ❏ Partially met goal
- ❏ Fully met goal

Recognition of possible issues that could involve the negotiator
- ❏ Did not meet goal
- ❏ Partially met goal
- ❏ Fully met goal

Psych consult considered or discussed
- ❏ Did not meet goal
- ❏ Partially met goal
- ❏ Fully met goal

Honest assessment provided to command post
- ❏ Did not meet goal
- ❏ Partially met goal
- ❏ Fully met goal

SCENARIO 18

Stalker, Workplace Violence

18 – Original Call

Report of shots fired at (location) with known victims. Suspect may have multiple firearms. The subject is at an unknown location inside the building. There are additional hostages. Patrol has responded. Set this up so it is NOT an active shooter situation. They have set up containment, and requested SWAT and HNT.

18 – The Incident: Escaped Witness Statements

AT 8:40 A.M. this morning, Minoru Suzuki entered the agency, and shot Vangie, one of the receptionists, in the shoulder, a relatively superficial wound. He then went into HR and killed the HR director and her two staff. He is somewhere in the building, heavily armed, with eight hostages. He has the hostages all in the same room, Vangie, among them.

Among the individuals who escaped are staff who know the layout of the building.

Minoru himself calls out immediately to the police on the phone. He says he wants to talk to a negotiator. He promises he will not harm anyone else, unless SWAT or other police attempt entry.

This is necessary to forestall this simply being an active-shooter scenario. This could be by telephone, to establish communications immediately that way, or, if you wish to have SWAT practice delivering a throw phone for example, have him begin just by yelling out to the police.

18 – Interview with the CEO of Your Local Mental Health Agency (and Notes for Role-Player)

Collaboration with a local mental health agency & Taking effective notes

As collaboration with mental health agencies always should be a priority for law enforcement, if possible, enlist the CEO to read/use this script over the phone. Given all this details here, one of the learning tasks of the interviewer will be to take good notes. In an after-action review, compare how much of what the CEO says (by referring to the script) with that in the notes that the interviewer actually takes down and what then makes it to the negotiation team.

Minoru Suzuki was employed at our mental health center as a case manager. He has an unusual history. Born in Vancouver, British Columbia, of Japanese immigrants, he is a Canadian citizen, and has lived in America with a Green Card.

As a teenager, he got into the hardcore Vancouver street drug scene. He was a heroin addict for seventeen years, this period only punctuated by several half-year binges on crack. At age thirty-two, he entered a drug treatment program and stopped using drugs altogether. Ever since, he has been totally 'straight-edge.' He won't even smoke cigarettes or have a beer.

Once he got clean, Minoru went immediately into therapy. He's thirty-six years old, four year's clean and not one relapse. He got certified as a drug-alcohol counselor, moved to the United States, and got hired as a street-outreach case manager. He is a wonderworker in the mental health and drug treatment systems. He can get rapport with any drug addict, he is fearless, and with seventeen years of survival practice on the streets of one of the meanest cities in North America, he can work the 'system' to his client's advantage better than any other case manager in the city.

We've observed a problem, however. It is a cliché that drug addicts stop maturing when they start using. Minoru started at age fifteen. So let's do the math. Gets clean at age 32, he's now got the emotional maturity, in some respects, of a late teen. The man is great on the street, but he is, per the women he's dated (some of whom work here) rather difficult. He is demanding, gets into passionate crushes towards various women, and then he gets possessive and jealous.

Minoru has asked out one of our receptionists. That's Vangie. She's a no-nonsense young woman who was, to say the least, not interested. She tried to let him down tactfully, but Minoru doesn't take 'no' for an answer.

I've got the notes from HR right here; let me read them to you. This was his approach.

You won't go out with me? Why not? Is it because I'm Japanese? C'mon, a little yellow fever would do you good. Hey, look, let's not call it a date. Let's call it: 'You go out with me for coffee and we see if we want to hook up after I tell you about my crazy life.'

No? Vangie, c'mon. Don't be like that. I'm beginning to think you might be a little racist or something. I mean, you went out with that white dude—Wesley. Whoa, whoa. O.K. I didn't know that was personal. I mean, he picked you up at work, I didn't know that was a sensitive topic. O.K. Look. Let me start over. Please? It's just—I never met anyone like you. I was on the streets, and those girls, they didn't respect themselves. You do. You have such class. You are different from them, and I just want a chance to know what I've missed after all the years I wasted. Vangie, I'm telling you—maybe you'll think I'm a little fast here, but you could be the ONE. . . . What? What! Well, you tell me this. WHY won't you go out with me then!

Vangie told him to stop, but it got worse and worse, and after the third such exchange, in front of clients in the waiting room, no less, she complained to HR. Minoru was asked in for a meeting, and the rules of workplace harassment were clearly explained. He was given a corrective action memo, and a warning. We told him if there were one more such incident, as highly as the agency regarded his work, he would be fired.

18 – Note to Role-player

This situation is so dangerous it already borders at the 'active shooter' level.

The only thing that keeps the police from entry is that you—Minoru—called them. You have got to keep talking. You will play him as a smart-ass, full of stories. You will mess with the negotiator, but must seem, in your own way, to be trying to work something out that will keep you from getting shot. Follow the coach's direction as to whether, at a certain point, you will escalate (to trigger a SWAT response), or if the negotiator finds something you are proud of, or think is worth living for, which would lead to your surrender.

18 – Psych Consult

Minoru fits a rather standard profile of the obsessional stalker. He has never been in a real relationship with the main victim. He was aware, unlike a psychotic stalker, she was not interested in him. He was not, like a sociopath, doing this for the thrill.

Obsessional stalkers get locked in towards the victim like a 'heat seeking missile.' It is very difficult for them to conceive of 'another way of looking at things.'

You should understand, however, that at least in the initial stages, they are not stalking to torment or terrify the victim. In the obsessional stalkers situation, not being with the object of their attention causes an unacceptable level of anxiety in the stalker. The anxiety is experienced as so noxious that it is better, perhaps, to die, than not 'have' her. In addition, because the victim, by refusing him, is the direct cause of his distress, the stalker perceives himself to be the victim. Therefore, their anxiety and distress often mutates into rage and hatred.

The negotiator is going to have a tough time with this individual:
1. He was a street criminal and drug addict. Police will not intimidate him, and he will be knowledgeable about police tactics.
2. He is a talker—interviews with staff who escaped as well other acquaintances, describe a fast talking, smart-ass, who likes to mess with authority.
3. He is committed. He's already murdered. What does he have to lose? It will be the task of the negotiator to engage him as long as it takes, to find what, if anything he cares about. Personal pride at being clean? His work? His integrity? The point is that the negotiator must connect him with the world of the living. <u>At this time, he's thinking apocalyptically—like Samson, in the Bible—bringing the world down around his ears.</u>

4. It is also the task of the negotiator, as much as possible, to keep him from focusing his attention on Vangie. If he does focus on her, he will very likely escalate, demanding either that she love him now, or that this is all her fault.

5. <u>One of the biggest questions you must ask is if he really has any demands</u>. Or is his intention to kill Vangie and others on his way out of this life?

6. Be aware the negotiator may make no headway with him whatsoever.
SWAT should be ready to move in at any moment.

SCENARIO 18 – Checklist for After Action Review

The after action assessment/critique will depend on what was expressed and expected of the team going into the exercise. In other words, what was the desired training goal or outcome? Not just the outcome of the scenario, but what are the skills the director (team leader) is hoping to see exercised by the team, as these scenarios/situations develop?

Floor plan developed quickly
- ❏ Did not meet goal
- ❏ Partially met goal
- ❏ Fully met goal

Demonstrate good listening skills
- ❏ Did not meet goal
- ❏ Partially met goal
- ❏ Fully met goal

Negotiator effectively de-escalated subject
- ❏ Did not meet goal
- ❏ Partially met goal
- ❏ Fully met goal

Psych consult recommended
- ❏ Did not meet goal
- ❏ Partially met goal
- ❏ Fully met goal

Honest assessment with command post/scene command/tactical commander
- ❏ Did not meet goal
- ❏ Partially met goal
- ❏ Fully met goal

SCENARIO 19

Dementia, Mercy Killing

19 – Original Call

Woman called, stating she believes her father is going to kill himself and her mother, using an overdose of Fentanyl patches…at…(location). Complainant will meet you there.

Upon arrival, house is locked up tight as a drum. Daughter does have a key, but when asked about weapons possession, she says her dad, does in fact, own guns. Patrol requests SWAT and HNT.

19 – Interview with Family Members Together

Information management—overlapping communication

This can be a good practice in managing information from several sources at the same time. People will not be belligerent, but they will talk over each other.

Complainant and other family members meet with officers. Their father, Benjamin, has initial stages of senile dementia. He is 86 years old. Their mother, Rivka, has 3rd stage liver cancer, and is under medical treatment. Doctors are not sure at this time if the chemotherapy they are using will be able to alleviate the cancer. However, she is not near death. "Our mom has always had a low pain tolerance, and she hates, more than anything, to be nauseated. She has three treatments to go, and the doctors say when they are completed, it will be a 'wait and see' situation. They say they will continue to give her pain medication, and they do have several options they haven't tried.

Rivka has received Fentanyl patches, and has, her daughter believes, nineteen left on her current prescription. Benjamin called this morning, in tears, saying he cannot stand his wife being in so much pain, and knows nothing will get better. He says Rivka has always taken care of him and the thought of being alone is frightening. "You'll put me in a nursing home."

He told his daughter he was going to put all the Fentanyl patches on the two of them and they would go to sleep in each other's arms, and be in Heaven together.

Rivka is not healthy enough to walk out of the house on her own.

19 – Interview with Daughter (HNT should separate her for more in-depth information)

The daughter states dad actually always controlled everything in the family, and he "is a Second Amendment gun nut. When he started showing dementia, we got pretty worried. He heard noises in the attic and shot through the ceiling one time."

She replies to what the officer says – "Yes, I know, we should have called you guys, but we didn't, O.K.? We're sorry."

Benjamin has had a lifelong obsession with government interference with privacy rights and gun ownership, and always stated the police would have to pry his guns from his cold, dead hands with a crowbar. Benjamin served in the military (two tours active duty in Vietnam, Marines). He was employed in a machine shop making tools, skilled labor, about which he was very proud. The shop closed and moved operations to Asia, something he's furious about.

19 – For the Role Players

Both will be on the phone – this will go back and forth. If you really want to make things complicated for the negotiator, have two phone lines, so that they will, often, both trying to talk at the same time.

Despite Benjamin's current cries of dependency—he has become somewhat childish with the dementia—Rivka is a very passive woman whose slogan throughout the marriage was, "<Sigh> "Whatever you think I should do, Honey."

Rivka will display a motherly attitude towards Benjamin, AND be passive-aggressive as well. She will, at various times, complain of severe nausea and pain, and this will wind Benjamin up.

Benjamin is going to be emotionally up-and-down, sometimes tearful, and sometimes angry in a blustery 'old-man's' way. To complicate things, he will show 'patchy dementia.' He will shift in-and-out of clear consciousness. This can be related, in part, to what food/water intake, to what memories are evoked, etc. He will lapse into reminisces of the past; he will forget what he verbally agreed to fifteen minutes ago and deny the negotiator and he had the discussion.

He does love Rivka and believes he is doing the best thing for her.

High-Register Tones/Voices and Old People

Be aware many elderly people have hearing loss, and usually the higher registers are the first to go. This can be a real problem if you are using female negotiators, who tend to have higher register voices (or a male with a high-pitched voice). In such a situation as this, if the subject IS having difficulty hearing, be ready to shift negotiators. (Perhaps you wish to offer a little 'in the field learning experience' to a negotiator who has a high-register voice who also happens to be a little too easily frustrated or irritated. Have the role player <NOT> hear or understand them. If the negotiator doesn't pick up on the hearing problem, he or she may get increasingly off-center. It then may be very productive to a) have a peer point out what might be the problem and see if they are able to hand over the lead, or if their ego keeps them in the chair b) transitioning to another lead negotiator and assessing how they handle it—first when they can't figure out why they are having a problem and second, after they understand).

19 – The Scene

Responding officers phone inside the house. Benjamin spoke to them and told them to go away. The officers will try to talk him into opening the door, saying they just want to talk, etc. Benjamin will threaten to shoot them. He will not brandish a gun, but will yell that he has several, and to prove it, will describe the make and type of gun and the type of bullets. Due to his mild dementia, he'll screw this up, which will frustrate him and make him angrier. Police will pull back, and set up containment.

19 – Psychological Consult

This is going to be a challenging negotiation. In the beginning, you should be trying to establish rapport. Get him talking about his life and marriage. Take notes so you are aware of what areas are sensitive to him—particularly what angers him. Put them on big-lettered notes on the wall, because talking to a contentious elderly person can be like a minefield. If he starts talking later about one of those areas, steer him away as soon as you can.

Due to his patchy dementia, he will forget what he agreed to. The negotiator's task will be to help him focus. Keep things simple.

Try to get Rivka on the phone. See if you can get her to stop complaining, and instead, to tell her husband she wants to go out and see their kids. You can also suggest she can advise him of some appointments she has scheduled. It is very possible, however, that Rivka will complain that you are asking her to lie to her husband, and will not say what you ask. Worse, she may complain to Benjamin about this.

One real risk of this situation is Benjamin is likely to be very stuck on the subject of his guns. If you focus too much on them, he will probably get completely obsessed about them, and there is a real danger that, upon surrender, he will want to go out with his guns in his hands. You will have to figure out a way – perhaps harkening back to securing weapons in the military—to get him to agree to leave without them.

One possible avenue, if you hit an impasse, particularly re surrendering the guns, is to ask him to talk with your sergeant about that. It is possible he may see the sergeant as a responsible party, whom he'll trust. **(Not lieutenant or captain—sergeant!).**

SCENARIO 19 – Checklist for After Action Review

The after action assessment/critique will depend on what was expressed and expected of the team going into the exercise. In other words, what was the desired training goal or outcome? Not just the outcome of the scenario, but what are the skills the director (team leader) is hoping to see exercised by the team, as these scenarios/situations develop?

Floor plan developed
- ❏ Did not meet goal
- ❏ Partially met goal
- ❏ Fully met goal

Demonstrate good listening skills
- ❏ Did not meet goal
- ❏ Partially met goal
- ❏ Fully met goal

How is the team dealing with the memory loss issues?
- ❏ Did not meet goal
- ❏ Partially met goal
- ❏ Fully met goal

How did the team deal with the issue of the firearms?
- ❏ Did not meet goal
- ❏ Partially met goal
- ❏ Fully met goal

How did the negotiator/team deal with the hearing loss (difficulty) problem?
- ❏ Did not meet goal
- ❏ Partially met goal
- ❏ Fully met goal

SCENARIO 20

Prison Hostage Taking, Rape

20 – Alert: Lockdown.

Barricaded inmate with a hostage. Kitchen admin office. Requesting immediate SWAT and HNT response.

20 – The Incident

Amos is a skinny kid, with no affiliation to any group within the prison system. As far as the administration is concerned, he's been a relatively quiet inmate—no critical incidents since his admission, two years ago at age 21. He had one administrative segregation bid after a confrontation with an inmate, and did six months solitary.

The prison is medium security. Amos has a job in the kitchen.

Today, he grabbed a corrections officer, put a knife to his throat, pulled him into a room off the main kitchen, and began screaming if it all had to end, he wasn't going alone. The officer in question has health problems—asthma and mild emphysema.

> **Construct a scenario regarding security that enables Amos to be barricaded, with no easy access to him.**
>
> There is real concern that any use of pepper spray or CS will be profoundly dangerous to the corrections officer due to his health concerns. The scenario can be set up purely as a negotiation or to include extraction, as needed.

20 – Information to be Revealed Upon Record Check

Amos Bosworth is 24 years old. He is incarcerated for 18—25 years for a murder. He was part of a group of three young men who decided to rip off their drug dealer. Although the robbery was successful, one of the young men got excited, and began pistol-whipping the dealer, who, seeing nothing left to lose, fought back. A third individual shot him.

20 – Character Instructions for Role Player

The negotiation is going to start with Amos in hysterical chaos. His demands make little sense. He wants 'out,' whatever that means. He wants to be left alone, whatever that means.

> ### Calm first, negotiate after
> The negotiator's initial job will be to calm down this hysterical man so he doesn't cut the throat of the officer.

20 – Further Information Provided by Intel

One to two hours into the negotiation, negotiators will get information that Amos got 'turned out' by one of the dominant inmates.

> ### Two alternative plot lines to choose from
> 1. Amos will NOT reveal that he was raped. If the exercise is played this way, the psych consult should suggest that the negotiator not raise the subject. Amos will play this as hyper-suspicious and he will 'project' – accusing the negotiator of being homosexual. If the negotiator is 'sensitive,' or too gentle/supportive in presentation, Amos will get more and more volatile and accusatory.
> 2. Amos will reveal he was raped. The negotiator should be respectful and tactful when s/he discusses this. If not, the role player should escalate dangerously. If the negotiator gets offended, dismissive, or otherwise doesn't get how volatile s/he is making things, escalate further. At this point, it'll be up to SWAT to save the hostage.

20 – Psychological Consultation

This may be a suicide-by-cop. Amos has taken a hostage, very likely, to force officers to kill him, to help him get 'out.'

GENERAL CONSULT

Amos is displaying a kind of 'paranoia'—he was overwhelmingly controlled by his rapist and his cohorts. He was also manipulated. If he perceives the negotiator as being too manipulative or controlling, he will most likely escalate. The negotiator should use the standard tactic with paranoia: a 'correct distance.' If the negotiator is too cold, officious or demanding, Amos will feel controlled (and possibly will attribute the coldness to his being judged) and he will escalate. If the negotiator is perceived as sympathetic or 'supportive,' Amos will see it as manipulative. It's very likely he will project onto the negotiator that he (or she) is homosexual. In this case, we are not concerned about political correctness; rather, the negotiator should matter-of-fact 'disengage' the subject. It's not about sex—this is about Amos getting help out of this desperate situation.

IF AMOS REVEALS HE WAS RAPED (BE PREPARED)

All of the above is in effect. The negotiator's task is must be two-fold: to offer a solution that Amos will be safe and get treatment for his trauma and secondly, to awaken his fighting spirit, that he will be helped to find a way to either get his rapists punished (without getting a snitch jacket) or, in general, do his part to fight prison rape. However, the negotiator should be acutely aware Amos could interpret surrender to power of any kind as another kind of rape, and he may push things to a lethal conclusion.

20 – What Amos will Tell If the Exercise is Set Up So that He Reveals that He's been Raped

Amos initially resisted, and the gang leader organized a gang rape. Because there were no severe injuries, Amos never presented at the infirmary. The leader gave his people strict instructions to "not damage his cherry. That's mine."

Amos thought if he fought back, he would be left alone. The rapes continued for nine days straight. He was frequently choked or smothered to unconsciousness, revived and raped and smothered again. He had the repeated experience of believing he would die.

After nine days, he gave in and became this man's 'wife.' He is not required to cross-dress in any manner, and would be beaten if he acted feminine. This is due to the rapist's aesthetic taste as well as his cunning. He keeps things under the radar. He lends Amos out, however, as payment for favors or debts.

He cannot sleep; he has a terrible flinch reaction to anything evoking thoughts of rape, or smothering. The smell of a particular hair product worn by one inmate or the smell of the disinfectant used to clean the floor that was on the rag stuffed into his mouth, causes panic reactions. Because these smells are pervasive, he believes his condition to be inescapable. He could smell it in solitary, and in addition, trustees used to come by the door of his cell and whisper the nickname "Little Bit," given to him by his rapist/owner.

Amos wants out. He wants escape, literally from his own existence, because everything in his existence—the smells, the sounds, the sights, re-evoke rape, not to mention the actual, ongoing rapes that occur.

SCENARIO 20 – Checklist for After Action Review

The after action assessment/critique will depend on what was expressed and expected of the team going into the exercise. In other words, what was the desired training goal or outcome? Not just the outcome of the scenario, but what are the skills the director (team leader) is hoping to see exercised by the team, as these scenarios/situations develop?

Floor plan developed
- ❏ Did not meet goal
- ❏ Partially met goal
- ❏ Fully met goal

Demonstrate good listening skills
- ❏ Did not meet goal
- ❏ Partially met goal
- ❏ Fully met goal

Negotiator must work hard to de-escalate
- ❏ Did not meet goal
- ❏ Partially met goal
- ❏ Fully met goal

Team must be aware of potential suicide by cop
- ❏ Did not meet goal
- ❏ Partially met goal
- ❏ Fully met goal

SCENARIO 21

Neighborhood Dispute, Bipolar

21 – Original Call

See the man regarding vandalism to his property. This address was flagged as a two officer response. The first officer arrived while his back up was still enroute. A few minutes later the officer broadcast: "Shots fired, shots fired!! Send more units." As other officers arrive, the original officer reports the following events leading up to the shots fired. They contain the house, and call SWAT and HNT.

21 – The Precipitating Incident

Today, Peter Janucek went outside to find the front of his house egged, and called 9-1-1. An officer went out to the house, a new officer just out of the academy. Peter began swearing at the cop for being a "jack-booted vegetable, who stands on my property looking stupider than my left ass-cheek, with no more utility than a prostate exam on a ninety-year-old woman."

The officer took it personally, and threatened to arrest him. Peter spat on the officer's uniform at which point he was sprayed in the face with pepper spray. Peter ran towards his house, screaming someone was going to pay. The officer tackled Peter, but he twisted free, kicked the officer in the face, knocking him out and ran into his house.

He emerged a moment later, fired a half-magazine with a semi-automatic at the house of the man he believed eggs his house, damaging a number of slate shingles, then emptied the rest of the magazine in the lawn around the fallen officer, who was just getting up, still dazed, from the kick to the face.

Peter, screaming, "Leave me alone," re-entered the house.

21 – Call to a Sergeant who is Familiar with Janucek

Peter Janucek is well known to police. He has bipolar disorder, and this manifests, in his case, in periods of social withdrawal, followed by episodes of mania (super high energy, grandiosity and irrational decision making). In his manic periods, he likes to dress up in very colorful clothes he has sewn himself, strips of different colored satin. He wanders the streets, singing songs to children, imagining himself to be a Teletubbie.

He talks very rapidly, and is usually funny. Some time ago, he accidentally overdosed on his medications. At the hospital, between bouts of vomiting, he was heard saying:

Why do you give a guy like me medicine that I can't be trusted to use properly? I can't remember what I had for breakfast, and you expect me to remember five pills taken three times a day? What is five into three, anyway? Why can't you give me Skittles? They've made some mistakes; I'll give you that. Those chocolate Skittles tasted like horsepucky. But I would definitely take Skittles every day if the doctor prescribed them.

He's not always funny, however. Like many manic-depressives, he has a hair-trigger temper and is easily irritated and thrown 'off-course.' And he has a neighbor who loves to torment him. Peter has clay shingles on his roof, and the neighbor, he alleges, occasionally uses a C02 gun to shatter one tile on random days. Peter has frequently called the police, demanding the police arrest the neighbor.

Police reports reflect a belief that the neighbor actually has done the shooting. However, the circumstances were always as follows: Peter would be outside, gardening perhaps, and suddenly he'd hear a breaking sound followed by the rattling of pieces of tile. No one was to be seen. Beyond evidentiary problems is Peter himself. What the police usually find when they come out is Peter on the neighbor's doorstep, pounding on the door, screaming in rage. He is incredibly frustrated with police because they won't "do something." He has made 78 calls to 9-1-1 this year, as well as a number of calls to the city council, the mayor and even the governor.

Police, after a consultation with a mental health professional have been urged to approach him with caution, and to guard their facial expressions. Peter's rants can be inadvertently funny, but he doesn't intend to do so—he can easily get offended and become enraged. This protocol was posted on the bulletin board, because they have so many contacts with him. The young officer was not aware of any of this.

21 – Interview with the Neighbor
The neighbor is a jerk, who speaks in a disrespectful manner to the police.

In past events, he's denied every accusation with a smirk. He likes to go as close to Peter's property as he can while the police are attempting to calm him down and wink at Peter, make faces and otherwise set him off.

This time is different. He's got scared when his roof was shot up, and the fear translates into shouting at the police to "lock the crazy bastard up." He will again deny any wrongdoing, and try to tell the officers they shouldn't waste time on Peter, he's just a fruitcake. And now that he's gone berserk, what are they going to do about it?

21 – For the Role Player
Peter will be initially ranting at the negotiator. He will be cursing and provocative. Though mentally ill, he's also sharp, and if he perceives he's gotten under your skin, he will drill in on you like a mosquito that just found a pulse. Even when you think you are making progress, he will 'jump sideways' into other subjects. If you get frustrated, he will definitely react to that as well.

21 – Interview with Another Neighbor

Peter is in the house with his developmentally disabled (Down's Syndrome) daughter, a sweet little girl, whom all the neighbors say he treasures.

21 – Interview with Peter's Wife

His wife returns home, driving up to see all the police. She says he's been very angry and despairing about the neighbor, and furious the authorities won't help. She is furious too (ROLE PLAY THIS). "For three years, we've tried everything, and all we get is mealy mouthed reassurance. It's your fault it's come to this."

She says he has not taken his medication for two weeks. The meds take several weeks to take effect when they are re-initiated. He has Xanax to calm him down in acute emergency states.

The wife is going to be righteously pissed off. She will be articulate, and not satisfied with empty promises or reassurances. What concrete actions can you take to help this situation, not just the barricaded subject incident at hand, but also the harassment by the neighbor?

21 – Psychological Consult

Although Peter is diagnosed with bipolar disorder, his behavior corresponds most closely at this time to what is called hypomanic. In other words, he is agitated, full of energy and volatile, but not totally raving. He is not delusional either.

The core problem, from his perspective, is he is not being taken seriously. He is not being heard. Tactical paraphrasing will be essential with this guy.

Do not start trying to focus him on his daughter until you have succeeded in paraphrasing. He must believe he's being heard, before he'll be willing to listen to you.

Because of his hypomania, however, this will be one step forward, two steps back. He will get distracted, will flame up at things, and suddenly shift into whimsical statements having little to do with the current situation.

SCENARIO 21 – Checklist for After Action Review

The after action assessment/critique will depend on what was expressed and expected of the team going into the exercise. In other words, what was the desired training goal or outcome? Not just the outcome of the scenario, but what are the skills the director (team leader) is hoping to see exercised by the team, as these scenarios/situations develop?

Floor plan developed
- ❏ Did not meet goal
- ❏ Partially met goal
- ❏ Fully met goal

Demonstrate good listening skills
- ❏ Did not meet goal
- ❏ Partially met goal
- ❏ Fully met goal

Important to demonstrate tactical paraphrasing
- ❏ Did not meet goal
- ❏ Partially met goal
- ❏ Fully met goal

Very key to demonstrate to this subject that he is being HEARD
- ❏ Did not meet goal
- ❏ Partially met goal
- ❏ Fully met goal

Consider calling in psych consult
- ❏ Did not meet goal
- ❏ Partially met goal
- ❏ Fully met goal

SCENARIO 22

Schizophrenia, Paranoid Delusions

22 – Original Call

Complainant calling, saying her ex son-in-law has broken into her daughter's home, and has her daughter and her two grandchildren at knifepoint. Officers respond and contain the house, requesting SWAT and HNT.

22 – The Incident

Josiah, carrying a large hunting knife, has broken into his ex-wife McKayla's, home. He is holding her and the two children, Cliff and Michael, aged three and four, at knifepoint. The children's grandmother escaped, but could hear Josiah shouting at the family through the window.

He yells he is going to cut the children's throats unless McKayla stops slandering him. Every time she denies it, he becomes more enraged. Officers can see him through the living room window. He currently has the knife in a sheath at his waist.

22 – Interview with the Grandmother

Josiah and his wife, McKayla, broke up three years ago. Since the breakup, Josiah, age 24, has been deteriorating. Approximately two years ago, he began brooding about his wife. He started calling her on the phone, and when she stopped answering, he began leaving messages, raving that she was laughing about him and lying that he lacked sexual prowess. The grandmother says she thinks he's 'psycho.'

22 – Role Player Planning

Josiah is going to answer the phone in a fury. He'll be raving, ordering the police to back off. He'll curse, and snarl how easy it is to cut a child's throat. He will say horrifying things about he'll bathe in the spray of blood, how he'll crack open their skulls and scoop out their brains and smear it in his ex-wife's face. He will push the negotiator's fears, so to speak, but as the negotiator starts the communication, he'll stay on the line rather than hang up and go after the kids. SWAT should be ready for a green light (and this case is excellent as a SWAT entry exercise as well).

If initial rapport is established, Josiah will begin to rave about what his ex-wife has done. He will start a litany of complaints about how she follows him, along with two guys who never say anything, but always stay two-and-one-quarter paces behind her.

Then, he will tell how six months ago, while he was trying to hook up with a young woman in a bar, he suddenly heard McKayla's voice, saying, "Girlfriend, you don't want to go home with him. He can't last, and anyway, he's hung like a mosquito." He whirled around, but did not see her. By the time he turned back from his room search, the young lady of his interest had started playing pool with another guy.

Since then, he has heard his wife's voice on frequent occasions, either when trying to pick up a woman, where, always, his sexual prowess and anatomy are derided, and also when he is anxious about something. He sometimes works for a tree topper, and now, when he climbs up, he hears McKayla laughing at him, saying, "Poor baby. Don't fall. You might break something. Not that there's much to lose, little man."

Josiah has never seen a counselor or psychiatrist, and has never taken medication. He absolutely believes the voice he hears is McKayla's and is absolutely real.

22 – Criminal Background Check

Three assaults: Two domestic violence attacks on McKayla (pled to assault four) and one fight. Regarding the latter, which occurred when he was seventeen, his opponent pulled a knife on him and he hit him in the temple with a rock. That would have been regarded as self-defense, but with the guy unconscious, he crushed both of his kneecaps and one elbow. He served three and one-half years in prison for that.

22 – Interview with a Friend

For this role-play, it would be productive to construct a crime scene, with a crowd. This gives an opportunity to practice crowd control and enact negotiations in a possibly chaotic situation, and also for collateral contacts to be searched for, and emerge from the crowd.

Unsolicited collateral contact

Here, the director can be innovative in how to introduce the 'friend' to the team. Maybe the friend shows up the barricade tape, as is often the case, offering to assist. Maybe the ex-wife mentions the friend has some insight into the subject's psyche. Maybe the director wishes to let this 'hang' for a while, and see if the team comes up with ideas to ferret out individuals who might have some interesting things to say about this subject that could prove helpful in developing his profile. This kind of scenario would be fun to let go for a while to see what ideas the team comes up with.

Police know the friend as a street thug. He lives around the corner, and has called in because "Josiah broke the code. You can fuck up a dude, and if your girl steps out on you, you gotta step up to that, but you don't scare kids."

He states he runs with Josiah, who is "fucking crazy, but stand-up. He will never back down in a fight." The friend is aware of the delusions, but "he calms down some when he drinks. "Give him a forty ouncer and things will go a lot better." The friend says, "What's kind of weird is Josiah gets straight about some things." When asked what that means, the friend says, "If you talk to him about his ex, his kids, most things, really, he's crazier than a shit-house bat. But if you talk to him about bikes (motorcycles—but he won't tell the negotiator that he means that instead of bicycles unless asked. If the negotiator start talking to Josiah about ten-speeds and mountain bikes, he will get more wound up), about fighting, and about John Carter of Mars (an Edgar Rice Burroughs science fiction series that they made a movie out of), he calms down, and is a cool guy."

Using a tablet reader to get information

With Kindle and other readers, the team can download one of the books he referred to. You may be able to talk about the book—if you are a speed-reader—to establish some rapport.

---

22 – Psych Consult Concerning Psychotic, Delusional Subjects

MOVE TOWARD AN ISLAND OF SANITY

Pay attention to subjects where the person is not delusional. Unless there is an emergent issue that must be addressed, divert your contact to those 'islands of sanity,' whenever possible, rather than allowing the conversation to focus on delusional subjects. Make links with other subjects not tainted by delusions. Think of yourself as expanding the size of the 'land-mass:' making an area where it's predictable and safe. If the individual gets stuck within his/ her delusions, you may find that changing the subject requires real finesse. Nonetheless, do so whenever you can, because talking about delusions makes it worse.

Islands of sanity are not necessarily 'nice' subjects

These islands of sanity are not necessarily 'nice' subjects. The consultant tells you s/he worked with a very dangerous man for nine months, and the only subject he could talk about without psychotic symptoms was bar fights. It was safer talking about the sound of a cue ball impacting on someone's skull than what he had for dinner or what his childhood was like.

TALK ABOUT THE DELUSIONS TO ASSESS RISK

Talk about the delusions as a means of threat assessment. Ask direct questions, particularly in regard to the person's intention to hurt him/ herself or others. When contacting such an individual, bring up the issue of concern yourself if they don't do so on their own, just to see if they have become seriously delusional again. For example, "The last time we talked, you told me about the Angel Michael and Satan. Are you worried about the Devil today?" Remember, the distinction between this rule and the previous two is that in this case, you are assessing risk, not just indulging in a conversation about their preoccupations.

DON'T AGREE WITH THE DELUSIONS

In almost all circumstances, don't agree with the delusions. At most, if you have a consensus among your team and consultant that it is worth the risk, passively accept their perception in the interest of their complying with something to keep everyone safer. This passive acceptance is almost never the best choice, however, so be very careful in its use.

DON'T DISAGREE—AT LEAST MOST OF THE TIME

Don't engage in arguments about whether the psychotic person's perceptions are real. However, if they ask you for a 'reality check,' you can state you don't believe the delusional belief is correct or the hallucination is real. In this case, you are helping the person understand what he/she perceives is not the "rule" of the world.

DIFFERENTIATE

Give the individual the 'right' to his or her own perceptions and beliefs. Inform them you don't perceive what they do, though you aren't arguing with them about what *they* see or believe. In some cases, take their delusions into account without agreeing with them. Example: "I don't see any razor blades on the tree branches, but if I did, I wouldn't walk around in the park after dark where I couldn't see what I might run into. I'd stay home when the sun went down."

STEAM-VALVING

This is useful with people whose speech is a cascade of words and ideas that are either all over the place (zigzag) or delusional.

- Listen and then interrupt, firmly but not aggressively.
- Sum up what they said, and tell them you want to hear more, but before they do, you have a question (or instruction) for them. For example, "Just a minute. I want to hear more about the fire in the eyes of crows, but first, tell me: Do you have a gun?"
- Then let them return to their cascade of words. Listen a bit more, then interrupt again. Continue with multiple sequences of release of pressure, interruptions and questions until you get the information you need.

Stay formal—do not get overly friendly!

Josiah is really paranoid. Stay formal, NOT too friendly. If he relaxes too much, he'll think you are messing with his head, and he'll go right back into rage.

SCENARIO 22 – Checklist for After Action Review

The after action assessment/critique will depend on what was expressed and expected of the team going into the exercise. In other words, what was the desired training goal or outcome? Not just the outcome of the scenario, but what are the skills the director (team leader) is hoping to see exercised by the team, as these scenarios/situations develop?

Floor plan developed
- ❏ Did not meet goal
- ❏ Partially met goal
- ❏ Fully met goal

Demonstrate good listening skills
- ❏ Did not meet goal
- ❏ Partially met goal
- ❏ Fully met goal

Did the team recognize the psych issues early on?
- ❏ Did not meet goal
- ❏ Partially met goal
- ❏ Fully met goal

Consider calling in psych consultant
- ❏ Did not meet goal
- ❏ Partially met goal
- ❏ Fully met goal

How did the primary deal with the delusional stuff?
- ❏ Did not meet goal
- ❏ Partially met goal
- ❏ Fully met goal

SCENARIO 23

Masked Depression, Intellectual Debate, Social Isolation

23 – Original Call

Complainant called stating she believes her brother is suicidal and is holding her two children without her permission. She will meet you a block from his residence at (location). (Radio also advises there was a call last night of a possible suicide at that same location…officers cleared, advising no contact was made). Patrol responds this time, and learns the following.

The sister knocked on his door, and the brother refused to open it, although he acknowledged he was inside with the children. He simply told her to go away.

What officers further learned from the complainant, caused them to request a supervisor and SWAT and HNT.

23 – The Circumstances Around the Incident: Interview with Sister

The role player should be highly emotional. She will be very upset the police did not force their way into Michel's house last night, and "Now he's more upset. It's your fault!"

Michel Chirac called up his sister, alluding to suicide last night. Police went to the house at her request, phoned him from their cruiser, received no answer and left.

Police Response to a Barricaded Suicidal Individual Where No One Else is at Risk

Based on a 9th Circuit Court of Appeals decision, police are not required to force their way into a house of a suicidal person if there is no risk to any other person. Different law enforcement agencies interpret this in very different ways. The writers encourage you to get clear legal advice from your own agency's counsel concerning this decision and its ramifications.

Michel saw the cruiser from the window and was deeply embarrassed. He called his family again, and said if the family name was going to be shamed, maybe the Chirac name should disappear. After an argument, Michel hung up the phone.

The next day, Michel went to the school of his niece and nephew, and picked the children up as they were walking home. When the children didn't return, their parents, frantic, called the school, who merely said the children had left at the regular time.

The parents called other children's homes and called Michel, because the children had, with their parents' permission, walked to his house after school on previous occasions.

Michel picked up the phone, said, "There is nothing more to talk about. I've already told you what needs to happen." He hung up the phone.

23 – Background on Michel Chirac: Interview with Husband of Michel's sister

If the training exercise is limited in scope, this could be a continuation of the interview with the sister. However, if the director of the exercise would like to enable another team member to practice interviewing a collateral contact, the role-player of the sister can become so emotional the husband steps in. One interviewer will use paraphrasing and reassurance to de-escalate the sister, while the 2nd interviewer can pull the husband aside, and gather information separately.

Michel Chirac is a doctoral candidate in political science. He's been working on his thesis for the past three years. His research is on the parallels between Biblical stories of the 'Promised Land,' and the concept of 'manifest destiny' in the taking over of the Old West in 19th century America.

The role player can use some other super intellectual set of ideas that s/he is familiar.

Aside from his research, he has no social life. For recreation, he has his television and his computer. He is obsessed with silent movies, and orders obscure Western (cowboy) 'classics' from an Internet source five times a week. His sister advises he owns several 'cowboy-type' guns, with which he practices his 'quick draw.'

He has not been on a date in six years.

23 – Initial Contact – For the Role Player

Negotiators make contact, and Michel will deny any intention to harm the children, but he will state he will not release them: "It is out of the question!"

Michel is going to present with a brittle arrogance, and intellectualization. The negotiator will be side-tracked over and over again as Michel will try to engage him or her in professorial debate on the state of the world, on philosophical and religious issues, and the meaning of life and a good name.

The role player should keep diverting the conversation back to your intellectual preoccupations. Occasionally, draw in philosophical questions about the meaning of life, and how suicide is considered in many cultures to be an act of intellectual integrity.

This will be difficult character for an amateur actor to role-play. You need to recruit a role player who has several hobbies or areas of public concern that he or she is really familiar: climate change, immigration issues, gun rights, the Bible, history of the old West, etc. The role player's presentation will be arrogant and for quite some time, disrespectful of the negotiator's knowledge.

23 – Psychological Consultation

Michel is resisting talking with you about the children because the conversation is an end in itself. He is desperately lonely and is striving to maintain conversation to barricade himself from the silence. He covers this up with his arrogance, and disrespect for your intellect.

<u>Important points:</u>
- Do not try to be smarter than he is when you are not—he will see through you.
- When you *are* smarter than him (when you know something he does not), do not try to prove him wrong, because if he loses, your dialogue is at an end. Do not be falsely humble, as he will see through that. Rather, draw him out so he can embellish his ideas and feel that he is making contact with another human being about something he loves.
- At the same time, do not suck up to him, giving him exaggerated respect for how much he knows, how smart he is.

Rather, present yourself with dignity and engage in dialogue. What I mean by this is a true dialogue is an exchange of truth back and forth, not a debate when someone wins and someone loses.

The crux of the matter is this, the longer and more solid the dialogue, the more you prove to him he is worth talking to. A person worth talking to is not alone. If you are successful in this, he will be 'pulled' back into the world of the living, where people have conversations with others, and feel a sense of hope for the future. Given he's made no overt threats, you may be able to minimize what he has done and encourage him to surrender.

Alternative outcomes to plan into this scenario

1. With sufficient dialogue, (a real challenge here), he surrenders.

2. By fully engaging him in conversation, he may get so wrapped up in the dialogue he loses awareness of what's happening around him and SWAT can enter and rescue the children. A great training task for SWAT would be silent entry. (Remember that he is a 'quick-draw expert.')

SCENARIO 23 – Checklist for After Action Review

The after action assessment/critique will depend on what was expressed and expected of the team going into the exercise. In other words, what was the desired training goal or outcome? Not just the outcome of the scenario, but what are the skills the director (team leader) is hoping to see exercised by the team, as these scenarios/situations develop?

Floor plan developed
- ❏ Did not meet goal
- ❏ Partially met goal
- ❏ Fully met goal

Demonstrate good listening skills
- ❏ Did not meet goal
- ❏ Partially met goal
- ❏ Fully met goal

Important that the negotiator realize he/she should not challenge this subject
- ❏ Did not meet goal
- ❏ Partially met goal
- ❏ Fully met goal

Consider using a psych consultant
- ❏ Did not meet goal
- ❏ Partially met goal
- ❏ Fully met goal

Important to have frequent status assessments with command post/tactical
- ❏ Did not meet goal
- ❏ Partially met goal
- ❏ Fully met goal

SCENARIO 24

Suicide of Cop by Cop

24 – Original Call

Neighbors reported shots fired at (location). Officers responded. Upon arrival, they reported, "Shots fired! Shots fired! Send more units! Request SWAT!"

This is the residence of Bernie Lawson, a sixteen-year veteran law enforcement officer. Tonight, he fired shots out of his window, hitting the house across the street. Police responded and he fired on the cruiser, hitting the hood. A perimeter was set up. He is well armed. It appears that he intends to force police to kill him. HNT is called to the scene.

24 – Background Information for BOTH Role Player and for Team

Bernie Lawson is a sixteen-year veteran law enforcement officer. About a year and a half ago, he was a first responder to a prowler call at the apartment of Sarah Donleavy. Sarah is the mother of two children, aged four and six. She had awakened in the middle of the night to see a man peering into her window. She hit the floor, and called 9-1-1. Due to the blind views around the apartment complex, he did not see the cruisers arrive and Lawson and several other officers arrested him, after a brief chase.

The perpetrator had a rape kit (break-in tools, rope, knife, and a collection of hard-core pornography). Further investigation revealed he had been stalking Sarah for some time. He had a past history of a rape conviction, as well as several other lesser predatory-type crimes against women.

Officer Lawson, who had established good rapport with the victim, came out to the house on several occasions to encourage her to prosecute, something she was, in her fear, unwilling to do. She eventually did agree to testify against the perpetrator. The perpetrator's family rallied around him, claiming it was a set-up by either Sarah and/or the police (they were never clear). The family made some public statements on TV, and they presented in a very threatening, but in no way legally actionable manner. Sarah, with her two young children, was terrified.

Sarah turned out to be a very overwhelmed young mother, abandoned by her husband. On several occasions, she ran out of food, and Officer Lawson bundled her and the kids into his car and rushed to the food bank so that she could get supplies before it closed. Fellow officers noted at the time that he was very concerned about her, but when they teased him a bit, he took offence. "I'm married, I'm forty five years old, and she's a single mom with two kids. Are you nuts? I just want to get this guy put away, and the young lady needs some help. If her life falls apart, will she show up for court?"

The perpetrator was convicted and is serving twelve years.

Officer Lawson, to the best of anyone's knowledge, was finished with the case. About three months ago, Sarah made a complaint of sexual harassment against him. She stated he dropped by the house late one night, ostensibly out of concern for her. He brought groceries. "One thing led to another," and he began kissing her. She was scared to tell him to stop, because she saw him as the only protection she had against the family of her attacker, and he was wearing a gun. He made statements that the police protect their own, and if she were 'his,' so to speak, her family would be far safer.

She stated he started coming over once or twice a week, for quickies. She did her best, she said, to fake it, because she was so scared for the safety of her children. With the perpetrator in prison and the trial well over, she felt safe enough to come forward to make him stop.

She presented photos, taken in her home of Officer Lawson and herself, next to the Christmas tree, and a few others with him playing with her kids. She had his cell phone number, knew his address, and the name of his wife. She also knew his wife had been hospitalized for depression, and stated Lawson told her that she had cut him off from sex, and that's why he was looking elsewhere.

Lawson denied everything. He said he'd helped her a few times, as described above, but he never went there for sex, never kissed her, never even thought of such a thing. Nobody believes him. His wife has left him. He's under investigation and has been taken off duty.

24 – Instructions for the Role Player

This role player probably *should* be a police officer, someone who is a veteran and very familiar with some of the grouchy, somewhat burned-out cops who perhaps have been on the job too long.

Lawson will talk with police. There will be opportunities for a variety of tactical exercises by SWAT to make this happen. He is going to be bitter and enraged. He will rant about how he's been betrayed by his brothers and sisters in blue, and he will be stunned his wife did not believe him. He will allude to suicide, and talk about taking an "honor guard to Valhalla with him."

This is a long barricaded situation. It should take considerable time to set up each interview, so the lead negotiator and SWAT are really working hard on this one.

24 – Interview with Wife

His wife refuses to give any information that might help resolve the situation peacefully, saying bitterly, "I don't want any of you to get hurt. Don't put yourself at risk for the son of a bitch."

The role player should make this a very challenging interview, in that she 'gives' nothing useful, but doesn't disengage. The interviewer could continue to talk with her for a while before realizing that, at least now, it is a waste of time.

24 – Interview with Sarah (Face-to-face)

This should happen at least several hours into the negotiation.

Sarah, hearing the information on the news, contacts the police. The role player can play this one of two ways: ONE—She will show far too much affection for Lawson for someone who has been, allegedly, villainously coerced into sex. TWO—She will be dramatic, accusatory and vindictive. In either event, however, her personal boundaries with the interviewer will be odd. She makes a lot of physical contact (doesn't matter if the interviewer is male or female). She is a little flirtatious, but when the officer asks her some hard questions about several things she claims, she flares up into anger.

24 – Contact with Sarah's Mother

Her mother informs the interviewer Sarah has always gotten crushes on older men. She was, allegedly, taken advantage of by a high school drama teacher. This incident ended his career. Her mother says, "I wonder if that was true, actually. He always denied it. She had a lot of details, even about marks on his body, but they were things you could see down somebody's shirt or with the sleeves rolled up. She had no description of any marks that would be on intimate parts. Oh, and you should have seen what happened when her husband left. They were married just a couple of years, it was a lousy marriage, really. Always fighting, those two. Well, he left, and she showed up at his new apartment, the third floor of a subdivided old house. He opened the door one morning, and there she was, sleeping in front of his door with the two kids in her arms. She'd broken a window in the door downstairs, opened the lock. Another time, he had a girlfriend up at his apartment, and she broke into the house, made quite a scene. Anyway, as soon as the divorce was finalized, he left the state. He said she was never going to let him go. He was no prize, and I feel sorry for the kids, but Sarah's a piece of work, actually."

24 – A Change of Focus

When this information is forwarded to the 'front line,' it definitely should change the focus of the negotiation.

This will **NOT** end the negotiation. It will just change its direction. Lawson is furious at IAD for not even admitting the possibility he was telling the truth, and is very cynical at this point. He will be suspicious the negotiator doesn't really mean anything he's saying, that it's just lies to get him to come out. It may be necessary to shift negotiators to get a fresh start. On the other hand, if the first negotiator can truly 'reboot,' this may prove to Lawson that someone actually believes him. The role player and director can drive this in either direction, depending on training agendas.

24 – Psychological Consult

Lawson is going to have to vent, in the classic sense of the word. Remember as far as he is concerned, no one has *heard* him. He feels completely discounted as the man that he truly is. The negotiator will have to prove to Lawson that he is truly heard, so tactical paraphrasing is going to be very important.

It's important the negotiator does not get defensive on behalf of the department or IAD. On the other hand, he or she must be careful not to stoke up/support Lawson's grievances.

Do not make the suggestion to reopen the investigation to clear his name too soon. The negotiator must assist Lawson in letting out the energy (the same way one slowly turns the cap on an over-heated radiator, let out a little pressure, pause, let out a little more pressure, pause, etc).

However, if Lawson simply vents 'in a circle,' there must come a point where the negotiator says enough. If such an impasse is reached, it may be effective to shift the call to a well-respected sergeant, who says, in essence, "Enough is enough. We have work to do to clear your name, and it's time we get started."

Scenario 24 – Make it a Successful Resolution

We recommend that this exercise results in a very tense, but successful resolution. SWAT's training will be in maintaining an absolutely safe scene against one who is familiar with police tactics, and making an 'airtight' surrender plan. The authors believe that a training scenario ending in the 'failure' of shooting a fellow officer, particularly one who is probably innocent of the allegations against him, would not be beneficial to the officers. We are not saying that it couldn't happen in real life—but we believe the team will be best empowered in this exercise with a success.

SCENARIO 24 – Checklist for After Action Review

The after action assessment/critique will depend on what was expressed and expected of the team going into the exercise. In other words, what was the desired training goal or outcome? Not just the outcome of the scenario, but what are the skills the director (team leader) is hoping to see exercised by the team, as these scenarios/situations develop?

Floor plan developed—from whom?
- ❏ Did not meet goal
- ❏ Partially met goal
- ❏ Fully met goal

Demonstrate good listening skills
- ❏ Did not meet goal
- ❏ Partially met goal
- ❏ Fully met goal

Are things handled differently because he is a cop?
- ❏ Did not meet goal
- ❏ Partially met goal
- ❏ Fully met goal

What about asking one of his friends, a fellow officer to assist? Useful? Good idea? Did the team consider it?
- ❏ Did not meet goal
- ❏ Partially met goal
- ❏ Fully met goal

Outside psych consultant considered?
- ❏ Did not meet goal
- ❏ Partially met goal
- ❏ Fully met goal

SCENARIO 25

Stalking – Revenge Suicide – Delusional Disorder

25 – Original call

Officers were dispatched to a suspicious circumstance. Check the welfare of the possible complainant at 9641 Wilmot. There is an open 9-1-1 line to that location—it sounds to the call-taker as if someone is being held at knifepoint.

Officers responded, contained the perimeter, and observe what they believe to be a hostage situation inside the home. Officer requested SWAT and HNT.

Information Acquired from a 9-1-1 Call Taker Who is Conveying Information Acquired from the Open Line from your Communications Unit

Rose Chen, a resident of Hong Kong, has invaded the home of Dr. William Stewart, her ex-professor. She is currently holding him at knifepoint. Stewart managed to thumb dial his cell phone to 9-1-1 and talking out loud, was able to apprise the dispatcher of the current situation. He stated, "I cannot believe you, Rose Chen, a former student, would enter my house at 9641 Wilmot Drive, Meridian, Idaho, and threaten me with a knife. I'm very frightened!"

Rewriting the plotline

As in other exercises, the director is quite free to rewrite the exercise to practice getting information regarding a subject from another cultural or ethnic group.

---

25 – Report of Investigating Detective (of Stalking Unit)

Rose Chen is a resident of Hong Kong. Seven years ago, she came to America and studied law at X University. She became obsessed with one of her professors, Dr. William Stewart. She took every class he offered, and applied to do her thesis under his supervision. He turned her down, as he already was supervising the maximum number of students he could manage.

Rose chose to interpret this as an announcement of his passion for her, assuming he did not want to mix any professional or tutorial responsibilities with the pure love they had discovered. She believed they had a secret pact, and she had to be circumspect, so that he was not accused of seducing or harassing a student. She began following him, running into him at social functions or public gatherings. It was then she realized that he was married.

This enraged her. His wife, aged 56, one year younger than Dr. Stewart, and looked every year of her age. How could he stand to spend any time with that woman, when he could spend every moment with her, Rose thought.

She began writing letters to Mrs. Stewart, claiming they were having an affair. A careful observer, Rose described gestures Dr. Stewart would make when laughing, how he pinched the bridge of his nose when he was tired. She observed the morning exercise routine he did in the backyard at five in the morning. She wrote to the wife how he was making progress with some of the exercises, and that they were going to start Pilates together. Mrs. Stewart, an insecure and jealous woman, believed the affair was happening, and confronted her husband. This was the first he was aware of Rose's interest.

Denying everything, he consulted with law enforcement, and following their recommendations, as Rose had not crossed the threshold of breaking the law, he tried to extinguish the behavior by ignoring her. He refused to greet her on the campus, returned all of her notes to his wife (retaining copies), changed his phone number and was altogether unresponsive to her.

When she began calling, he hung up. Unfortunately, his wife was not able to maintain, and on her own, went to Rose's apartment to sit down and talk with her. It did not go well. Rose convincingly described their lovemaking, with such assuredness and graphic detail, that Mrs. Stewart was convinced it was true. It didn't help their own relationship in that area was troubled. . . actually non-existent. Mrs. Stewart slapped her face, but Rose only smiled sweetly at her, and suggested if she moved out, it would be better for all concerned. Mrs. Stewart believed her and moved out of the house, initiating divorce proceedings.

Integration of Other Units in the Scenario

The authors recommend using a staff member from your communications division to play the part of the 9-1-1 call-taker, and a detective who specializes in this type of case. If your department has such a detective, recruit him/her to be on your training committee to develop this training. Ask the detective to assist in developing this script based on a case they may have handled. Then, ask the detective to play him or herself, responding to the scene to provide the background on the subject, to reveal what would be known from the police reports. Of course, this would be after the team discovers there is a history to be revealed.

It is generally good practice to involve police units, who may actually become involved in SWAT/HNT situations, in role-plays. Get them involved in the practice scenarios, so they know what is expected of them, and the HNT knows what resources and skills they can bring to the table.

---

25 – Further Information from 9-1-1 call taker listening in on the open line recording conversation between Dr. Stewart and Rose.

From what was relayed, it appeared as though Rose waited a few weeks and went to the house. Finding it locked, she broke in and greeted Dr. Stewart naked in his now lonely bed. He was not pleased. In fact, he was terrified. Grabbing his bathrobe, he ran for the door with Rose blocking his way. At this point, she pulled a knife and slashed her own cheek, saying she was ready to die for their love. And she knew he is willing to die with her.

25 – Parents in Hong Kong – Interview

> ### Getting information from overseas—both in fact, and in the interest of an effective training scenario
>
> This presents a problem solving effort for the team to practice. How would they make contact with someone overseas, if they did find a contact number for Rose's relatives? (The exercise can be set up so that the contact number can be secured from school records, a roommate, friend or employer—depending on available resources, and on whether the team leader wants to set up a small collateral interview with the informant)

The parents state she had a previous episode 12 years ago, when she was similarly obsessed with a professor. She stabbed him. Then a minor, she was placed in a psychiatric hospital, and responded to a regimen of anti-psychotic medications. The medications were discontinued after one year of treatment and she's had no further episodes. The parents state their daughter truly believed that the professor loved her, and she would 'twist' anything around into a positive meaning. For example, two days before she attacked him, she accosted him on the street, and he, frightened and fed-up, punched her. She returned home, smiling, telling her mother she now knew that the professor loved her, because love was a test. "There is no rose without thorns," she said. "I will prove to him that no matter what the test, I will rise to meet his love." When she assaulted him, she intended to kill him and commit suicide, because she believed they were destined to live together in Heaven. The parents note they are Christian.

25 – Cultural Consult

If possible, access someone familiar with Chinese culture. Remember, she is from a very upper-class family. Although Christian, she will very possibly subscribe to traditional Confucian values, particularly filial piety.

Effective Use of Cultural Consultation—and Effective Cultural Consultants

It is important that you have a cadre of consultants who are able to discuss both cultural rules, and exceptions to the rules. For example, if the subject does not seem to conform to the cultural rules that the consultant expects, they should be willing and able to brainstorm with you why the subject's behavior seems to be atypical.

---

25 – Instruction for the Role Player – Rose

You will be highly educated. It may be a worthwhile addition to the exercise that you have a heavy accent, but this is only valid if the accent is well played. If you shift in and out of character or you are unskilled, it will make the training exercise sound ridiculous and unreal. You will speak about your 'relationship' in fixed sureties—it is absolutely the truth. You will be kind of smug.

25 – Instruction for the Role Player – Stewart

You will be attempting to feed more information to 9-1-1 through your 'running commentary' with your hidden cell phone.

25 – Examples of By-play Between the Role-Players Overheard by 9-1-1

EXAMPLE #1

Stewart – "I can't believe you would walk into my house, with no respect for my privacy. Here I am, naked, except for a bathrobe, and you threaten me with a knife."

Rose – "There is no shame between lovers. I think you have a beautiful body."

EXAMPLE #2

Stewart – "What are you going to do with that knife?"

Rose – "When we are married, I will use it to cut vegetables for your dinner."

Stewart – "I am married! Leave my house right now."

Rose – "You are being silly. Of course we are married. You come to me in my sleep and caress me. It is very mean that you would lie to me now, after what you have done to me in the dark. If you think you must lie to me about our love here on earth, we can be married together in Heaven. I can cut the bonds of life that tie you to that silly fat woman."

EXAMPLE #3

Stewart – "Could you open the drapes. It's dark in this living room. I have a large window and it is lovely outside. I want to see the sky."

Rose – "Why would you try to trick me like that! I am not stupid! You don't have to play games and torture me any more. I have proved my love already!"

25 – Psychological Consult

Ms. Chen truly believes the professor loves her. You will NOT be able to argue her out of this. Evidence will prove nothing to her. Argumentation will agitate her.

The negotiator should get her talking, using paraphrasing and open-ended questions. Allow her to talk about their love, but every time she starts talking in apocalyptic or self-destructive terms, steer her back to talking in more generalities about love. The goal is for her to experience a sense of acceptance, <u>without</u> any explicit validation of her claims. Your hope is by being allowed to talk about this without the resistance she expects, SHE may concoct the idea she can surrender, and the world will be accepting of her. However, remember she has a fixed locked-in delusion. It is quite possible you are merely speaking with her to fatigue her and buy time so SWAT can enter, or Dr. Stewart is able to escape.

Do NOT forget that Ms. Chen is paranoid—yet very intelligent. Like a porcupine, she will have hair-trigger defenses. Do not be too familiar/friendly with her, because she will be suspicious you are trying to get under her defenses.

Feel her out on what her parents may feel about the current situation, but do NOT try to hammer her with an obligation to her parents. However, it is possible she may veer to thinking about the effect on her parents, and on her own, decide to 'use' her love for her parents to persuade herself to surrender. Follow her lead! This could be risky, if her parents' response to her last incident was punitive or shaming.

SCENARIO 25 – Checklist for After Action Review

The after action assessment/critique will depend on what was expressed and expected of the team going into the exercise. In other words, what was the desired training goal or outcome? Not just the outcome of the scenario, but what are the skills the director (team leader) is hoping to see exercised by the team, as these scenarios/situations develop?

Floor plan developed
- ❑ Did not meet goal
- ❑ Partially met goal
- ❑ Fully met goal

Demonstrate good listening skills
- ❑ Did not meet goal
- ❑ Partially met goal
- ❑ Fully met goal

How did the team deal with the issue of necessary overseas contact? Is there a plan/practice in place for the future?
- ❑ Did not meet goal
- ❑ Partially met goal
- ❑ Fully met goal

Cultural consult necessary?
- ❑ Did not meet goal
- ❑ Partially met goal
- ❑ Fully met goal

Psych consult?
- ❑ Did not meet goal
- ❑ Partially met goal
- ❑ Fully met goal

SCENARIO 26

Impulse Control Disorder: Possible Neurological Impairment
Due to Possible Pre-Natal Drug or Alcohol Use

26 – Original Call

Reported disturbance at a coffee shop. Customer is intimidating and threatening to other customers. Upon officers' arrival, they observed customers fleeing the store, also observed a male holding a female at knifepoint. Officer's requested SWAT and HNT.

26 – Witness Accounts Including One First Responder

There will be multiple interviews—three or four—should gather the following composite information. Each witness should present with somewhat different emotions: angry, scared, stunned, or clear and cooperative.

A young man went into a coffee shop and ordered a double caramel latte with sprinkles. When an older man snickered towards his wife that a young man would order such a girly drink, the subject turned around in the line, fixed him with a stare for a very long minute, the elderly gentleman getting more and more nervous.

The aggressor said, "You have something you want to say to me directly?" The man shook his head. The aggressor turned to the nervous barista, said, "Wait a minute, darling," and walked back to the man, put his arm around his shoulder and said pleasantly, "Seems you think I'm some kind of faggot based on the kind of coffee I drink. Should I fuck your wife to prove you wrong? How'd you like that darling', you want to feel young again?' The two of them tried to avoid eye contact. The aggressor pinched the man's cheek with his thumb and forefinger, digging in the nails until the man's eyes started watering. He released him, patted him on the cheek and said, "Don't worry, we're just getting a little more acquainted, aren't we. In the future, don't sell tickets with your crocodile mouth that your bumblebee ass can't cash."

He strutted back past the stunned customers, and went to take his drink. When the barista put it on the counter, he said, "That's rude, honey. You should hand a man his drink." She did, but it was very hot, and she was so nervous by this point that she let it slip and the scalding liquid went all over his hand.

The aggressor exploded, throwing the rest of the coffee in her face. When one man behind him grabbed his shoulder, he turned around and punched him in the throat.

Meanwhile, while this was going on, the elderly man whom he had originally bullied had called the police. A cruiser was nearby and they pulled up just as the aggressor punched the man in the face. Customers started running out just as the police were trying to enter, blocking them. One of the officers hollered at him to stop and the aggressor's response was to whip out a jagged clip-it knife, vault the counter, and yell at the cops to back out or he'd cut the bitch's (barista's) throat.

The scene, static, consisted of the aggressor behind the counter with the barista as a shield. When one cop began to move forward, he made a small slice in the girl's neck, pulled the knife away, and said, "She lives if you back out. Come forward and she dies. I don't give a fuck about me. Ireland rules!"

26 – Criminal Background Check

This is difficult for the team, because determining his identity could be problematic. Usually these guys do not give up their first and last names readily. This is where the director of the exercise can be creative. Perhaps one of the responding officers had handled this kid recently, and had notes regarding the contact. (That's the easy way) Did anyone see him exit a vehicle that could be checked? Did he work nearby, and someone at the coffee shop can place him as an employee at a nearby business? Sometimes the information comes from a helpful person at the 'yellow tape,' especially when a call involves street people. Once a scene has been cordoned off, and the crowd gathers, if the crowd can see the subject, there is almost ALWAYS someone who will recognize him/her and provide some information on them. When dealing with street people, the information might be "Oh, that guy hangs out at such and such mission" or, "Yeah, that guy is known as "Eamonn" or "Mad Dog" (or whatever) At least that usually gives you a starting place to begin the identification process. Remember, for the negotiators, it never hurts to ask the subject for their name. Sometimes, of course, they are proud to give you their name.

Criminal background check, by whatever means it is acquired, reveals Eamonn Caffery, a twenty-five year old male. His record shows seven misdemeanor assaults since his sixteenth birthday. Further inquiry reveals each of them was a plea bargain. The actual assaults were far more serious, but each time, various prosecutors pled him down. Eamonn was also repeatedly violated while on probation. His probation officer recalled him as someone whom he'd only meet with another officer nearby. Eamonn always got infuriated by anyone telling him what to do. He's always bragged about his 'Irish temper,' although he's adopted from fifth generation Americans.

Beyond identity—following leads for more Intel

Along with figuring out how he is identified, the director needs to determine how the negotiators are going to follow leads to find his sister and his parents to gather the additional information. Remember, this all needs to be figured out ahead of time. The director should have a plan, and, if necessary, you might have to make training suggestions to your team to assist in moving the scenario along, if it gets stagnated because they are not developing the right Intel. Please remember to be open to other ideas for collecting Intel, and finding sources, however.

26 – Interview with Sister

"Eamonn was adopted. All we know about his mother is that she was really wild, and used a lot of drugs."

He was expelled from five different schools, always for fighting. He has a history of taking offense easily, particularly when he is confused by what someone is staying. The doctors suspected both fetal alcohol and intrauterine methamphetamine exposure.

His sister reports," He always feels stupid. But he always has had this prepared speech: "You can look at someone and think: 'That's an interesting idea. You are probably right. But that doesn't change the fact that I can kick your fucking ass, and you can't do anything about it. Think your way out of that, smart guy.'"

Everyone knows he carries a knife. He loves flashing it, and he cut one other boy in high school. It was a three-on-one confrontation, Eamonn had beaten up one of the boy's brothers, but technically speaking, they started the fight that led to the knifing.

26 – Interview with Father and Mother

His father says, "After one of his explosions, he always feels awful about what he's done. Really. He's cried in front of me. But in the moment, it's like something takes over him. He tells me he 'reds-out,' and hardly remembers what happened."

His mom says, disagreeing somewhat with his father, "I have no doubt Eamonn does 'red-out,' as he puts it. But my son hates other people whom he thinks might be smarter than him. He's a bully and a thug. I hate to say it. Yes, I think his remorse, which he sometimes has, is genuine, as far as it goes, but bullying people is his addiction. If he backs into a corner, I think he will cut that girl. And one final thing, you need to tell the girl to somehow be strong and calm! He hates weak people most of all. If he thinks she's whiny or scared, he will hurt her badly."

26 – Instructions for the Role-Player – Eamonn

You should play this character as loud, defiant and boisterous—a bully with a smile. Any time the negotiator uses a long, complicated sentence or big words, you will get confused and angry. When you want to understand something s/he is saying, you will ask:

- What the fuck are you on about?
- Are you making fun of me? What the fuck does that mean?
- Talk like a fecking (remember, he pretends to be Irish) human, professor.

Your temper is going to flare up suddenly and very loudly. When frustrated, you will threaten the hostage, loudly, even screaming, "You want to see this girl bleed?" "How do you think she'll look if I give her a second smile?"

26 – Instructions for the Role-Player –The Hostage

You are going to be very scared. At various times, you may beg him to let you go—*while he's speaking to the negotiator.* He is going to get enraged at that. If/when the negotiator conveys to you how important it is to be strong, make yourself a brave, dignified young woman who is captive in body, but not in mind. No matter what happens, you will not lose your integrity. Do not treat him with contempt or defiance— just quiet dignity.

26 – Psychological Consult

Even psych consults need to consult

Given the reports, Eamonn probably has some kind of neurological damage, resulting in intellectual impairment, and impulse control problems. Your usual psych consult may know about this subject, but maybe not. A good training exercise for your own psych consultant would be to access a specialist in this area to give you more information.

Eamonn is reported to have an explosive temper, somewhat limited intelligence, particularly in the realm of abstract thinking or imagining future alternatives. Based on history, there is a probability he is neurologically impaired, based on pre-natal drug/alcohol use.

The officer must be matter of fact, not 'warm and supportive,' which Eamonn will perceive as either weakness or manipulation. On the other hand, if Eamonn perceives the officer as talking down to him, or trying to order him around, he will escalate.

The officer should, if possible, try to speak to the victim directly to be strong and calm: she should not beg, but at the same time, not express any contempt. Of course, this will be difficult to do, but if an opportunity presents itself, she should be encouraged that way, perhaps through the hailer. For example: "Angela, we are discussing things with Eamonn so we can hopefully get an agreement with him to release you. You will help us greatly if you stay calm, and let us talk with this man so he doesn't have to be distracted."

Alternative endings

- A surrender (this will be difficult because of a) his information processing problems b) his temper and impulse control
- A surrender that suddenly changes into an assault (impulse control again)
- SWAT enacts a hostage rescue (signals and in-the-moment communication with the hostage could be a great exercise to coordinate with HNT)
- SWAT sniper training

SCENARIO 26 – Checklist for After Action Review

The after action assessment/critique will depend on what was expressed and expected of the team going into the exercise. In other words, what was the desired training goal or outcome? Not just the outcome of the scenario, but what are the skills the director (team leader) is hoping to see exercised by the team, as these scenarios/situations develop?

Floor plan developed
- ❏ Did not meet goal
- ❏ Partially met goal
- ❏ Fully met goal

Demonstrate good listening skills
- ❏ Did not meet goal
- ❏ Partially met goal
- ❏ Fully met goal

Did primary keep the subject calm?
- ❏ Did not meet goal
- ❏ Partially met goal
- ❏ Fully met goal

What ways did Intel come up with to ID the subject?
- ❏ Did not meet goal
- ❏ Partially met goal
- ❏ Fully met goal

SCENARIO 27

Sadistic Violence, Hostage Murder Threat

27 – Original Call

See the school counselor who has a student who wants to report involvement with a serious crime. Officer responded, learned the following, which developed into a SWAT/HNT situation.

27 – Background – Interview with School Counselor (Brandon, tearful, is sitting in the counselor's office)

Brandon approached a school counselor and asked if he could talk about something that had been bothering him. He asked if the counselor could keep it secret. The counselor explained the rules of confidentiality: she would be required to report an act of intended violence, abuse of a child, etc. Brandon dashed out of the office. The counselor followed him out and found him slumped, with his head in his hands, on one of the bleachers. Brandon, she was aware, is a 'latch-key' kid, with an absent father, and a mother whom she describes as a 'cold refrigerator.' "She has never, in any teachers' knowledge, said or done anything affectionate to Brandon." The counselor sat down beside Brandon, and he burst into tears.

He told her he and his three friends had, about six months ago, picked up a girl who was hitchhiking. "You know, the girl on the telephone poles?" She was taken to William's house, up to the third floor, and since then, kept as a prisoner. The school counselor then told Brandon that he needed to be talking to police about this, and s/he promised to get help for him.

27 – Interview with Missing Person's Officer

> **Integration of Other Units in the Scenario**
>
> The authors recommend using an officer from your missing person's unit or a detective who would be involved in a case like this. It is generally good practice to involve police units, who may actually become involved in SWAT/HNT situations, in role-plays. Get them involved in the practice scenarios, so they know what is expected of them, and the HNT knows what resources and skills they can bring to the table.

The only girl whose picture is on telephone poles in recent days is Melissa, a chronic runaway. Her mother used drugs, and brought boyfriends home, one of whom, it was known had molested her. Her counselor described Melissa as 'acting out.' She was both sexually promiscuous and used drugs, just like her mother. After an investigation, the police stated all components seemed identical to her three previous runaway attempts. A backpack and some clothes and two bottles of vodka were missing, and a curse written in lipstick on the walls. They assumed she had actually made it to the city and was living on the streets or in a shelter somewhere. Her mother refused to believe this and continued to plaster the small town with "Have you seen this child?" posters on telephone poles and store windows.

27 – For the Role Player

Brandon should be played as very emotional and remorseful. He starts off as unresponsive, however, to direct questions. If the interviewer is harsh or demanding, Brandon will get a little defiant as well.

Alternative plans for how to work with Brandon
- **In the interest of time, the negotiator can successfully get through Brandon's initial defenses**
- **If preferred, the interviewer should quickly get a psychological consult (or this can be presented as the result of a hypothetical phone call to a consultant to assist in the interview).**

---

27 – Psychological Consult Regarding Brandon #1

Brandon desperately wants to be reassured that he is OK. He should be interviewed much like the preliminary steps in the Reid method (NOT the 2nd level interrogation).[6] The interviewer is warm—he or she must find something to like in Brandon, and *emotionally* convey this, like a warm, firm uncle or aunt. The interviewer should 'contextualize' what Brandon has done: "You did the best you could:" "That must have been really hard for you." "You were trapped:" etc.

27 – Brandon's Information

William, Andrew, Brandon and Greg, sixteen and seventeen years old, have been friends for several years. They bonded around computer gaming, and have been enthralled by increasingly violent games, culminating in cop killing/kidnapping/gratuitous killing such as Grand Theft Auto. Additionally, they got interested in pornography, and this, too, became progressively violent. They discovered violent bondage and torture sites on the internet, which take things to extremes of either simulated, coerced or even 'agreed' to activities including degradation, shedding of blood, suffocation, mutilation, etc. They've been searching for real 'snuff' films.

William is the alpha of the group. He has unlimited freedom, because, after his mother and father died, he was raised by an aunt who, in his teen years, has become mildly senile. William has intimidated her to the degree she does not go to the upper floors of the three-story house. Over several years, William has

---

[6]   http://en.wikipedia.org/wiki/Reid_technique

frequently screamed at her, struck her, and played music at top volume. With no other houses in near proximity, there have been no neighbors to complain.

About six months ago, there was a mysterious incident in town. A single mother, who has had a rather problematic history of her own, reported that her daughter, aged fifteen, had disappeared.

Brandon describes he and his friends picking up Melissa, who was hitchhiking and taking her to William's house.

She was fed one meal a day, and the four boys, for the past six months had been raping and torturing her. "William's the one who thinks most things up, but the other guys do to. Like, once when Andrew was, um, doing things to her, William made her start singing, 'I will survive,' and when she stopped or screamed or stuff, he would cut her, just a little, with his knife. She had to thank him and start over." They played music very loud over her screams, and the aunt, used to loud music and the violent cackling of vicious teenaged boys from the upstairs, just tried to ignore it.

Brandon minimized his role, both to the counselor and to the police, but he is apparently being less than honest. He, the runt of the group, desperately wanted to be included. What will 'leak out' in his account is that he was excited to be part of this, but he grew to hate Melissa. When the other guys pushed him to do something sexual in front of everyone, he had problems performing. He got a new nickname from his friends: "Limpdick." He began to feel that it was Melissa's fault, because, if she hadn't been there, he wouldn't be in the situation he was in. Out of hatred and also to prove to the guys that he was with them, he enacted spontaneous brutality of his own, so he wouldn't be teased, victimized or cast out.

Two things intervened: He heard a televangelist on TV, and he actually listened. Instead of talking about prosperity, this preacher was talking about sin, and how, no matter how bad the sinner, the Lord would accept him or her, if there were true repentance. Brandon wanted to be free of the sick disgust and fear he perpetually felt. Secondly, the girl was getting sick. Some of her wounds were septic; she was malnourished and had lost the will to live. No matter how they hurt her, she just whispered, "Finish it. Just finish it." This was actually intimidating to two of the guys, who were weaklings and were living off of breaking down her will. They didn't know what to do with someone with nothing left to lose. William would casually use her as a punching bag, but his sadism had no outlet.

Brandon stated, "She's going to die, and they are going to bury her somewhere. Soon, I think. I just want to get clean. I can't get the smell off of me. She smells like spoiled meat. She looks really bad."

One final salient point – Brandon said that William really was into Grand Theft Auto and fantasized a lot about killing a cop and going out in a blaze of glory. He owns two automatic handguns, and a shotgun. "Andrew's stupid, he just does what he's told, and Greg is too weak to ever go against him."

27 – Psychological Consult – #2

As rapport is built, the interviewer will, of course, begin to ask questions about the house layout, what makes each of the boys tick. As this goes on, if the interviewer is able to establish a 'benign dominance' over Brandon, he should strive to get information on how to separate the other two boys from William. Brandon should feel he is helping by explaining the dynamics between the boys. He can, thereby, feel a small sense of power over the others, who call him "Limpdick." If he expresses enough *open* resentment, the interviewer may share a feeling of outrage on his behalf, that maybe it's a mark of a healthy <u>man,</u> that he doesn't get hard with a girl in those circumstances. Be careful though—it is possible that Brandon was sexually excited, either by the torture or by having sex in front the other boys. Let Brandon take the lead, because if you ally with what he is saying and not what he is really feeling, he may shut down before you get enough information.

27 – The Scene

Police attempted to enter the house, but were seen by one of the boys, who fired through the door with the shotgun. They have pulled back, established a defensive perimeter, and have begun negotiations. The girl is grabbed by the hair, shoved half out the window, and one boy yells she will be shot "like they do to bitches in the Congo," if the police try to enter and rescue her.

Everything is important! Do your research!

Every phrase by a hostage-taker may be significant. If they do some research—and Google/Bing and Wikipedia make it easy—it won't take long for the team to know what has happened to women in war-zones in the Congo.

---

27 – For the Director and Role Players

What makes this situation especially complex is William orchestrates the conversations with the negotiator. He trades the phone off with the other two boys. William does NOT direct them. It is almost as if he is curious to see what each of the boys will do and how the negotiator will approach them. He is on speakerphone—start by using the home phone—so he listens in on everything said, and the negotiator has a hard time trying to split off one boy from the other.

Behaviors of the role players:
- William is not as smart as he thinks he is, but he will be provocative and insulting. He will taunt the police, and at various times, as previously, show Melissa in the window and threaten to hurt her. He won't do anything, however, that would necessitate immediate SWAT entry unless/until you wish the exercise to go in that direction.
- Andrew will be played as an unintelligent guy who tries to be tough.

Greg will be the pliable one: he will ask William what to do or say. If the negotiator is successful, Greg will shift dependence over to the negotiator, who will try to make him feel that the police can help him out of this dead-end situation.

Alternative Training Goals

1. Joint SWAT/HNT – This could be an excellent scenario for a joint SWAT/HNT exercise, with the goal of taking out the victim takers, and rescuing the young woman.

2. Splitting off one hostage taker – It would also be an excellent complex scenario, where you figure out how to 'split' Greg off and maybe work in your favor.

SCENARIO 27 – Checklist for After Action Review

The after action assessment/critique will depend on what was expressed and expected of the team going into the exercise. In other words, what was the desired training goal or outcome? Not just the outcome of the scenario, but what are the skills the director (team leader) is hoping to see exercised by the team, as these scenarios/situations develop?

Floor plan developed
- ❑ Did not meet goal
- ❑ Partially met goal
- ❑ Fully met goal

Demonstrate good listening skills
- ❑ Did not meet goal
- ❑ Partially met goal
- ❑ Fully met goal

Interview with Brandon (the witness) is key…how was that handled? Specialist called in?
- ❑ Did not meet goal
- ❑ Partially met goal
- ❑ Fully met goal

Important to discuss options with tactical while this is developing
- ❑ Did not meet goal
- ❑ Partially met goal
- ❑ Fully met goal

SCENARIO 28

Hostage Taking in the Commission of a Crime
Devolving into Suicide by Cop

28 – Original call

Silent alarm at a bank. Responding officers arrived, and reported seeing a man inside with hostages, brandishing a weapon.

Perimeter was set up, SWAT and HNT requested.

Working with the FBI

Anytime you have a bank robbery, FBI is going to respond. This is the perfect opportunity to do some joint training with the FBI hostage negotiators. If you have not already made connections with your local FBI field office, particularly their negotiating team, this is a good exercise to get them involved in. The truth is, the FBI negotiators really enjoy working with the local law enforcement on training exercises. They learn as much from local law enforcement as locals do from the FBI. Furthermore, if there is a bank robbery, it will be joint jurisdiction, so you are apt to have a situation with FBI negotiators working alongside the local law enforcement negotiators. If you have already met and figured out how to work together, such collaboration will go smoothly.

---

28 – Note for the Role Player – First Section

Identification (For HNT)

The director needs to determine how the problem of identification of the subject is going to be overcome. Did the subject drive a car? He may not want to identify himself right away, but don't give up on that. Ask him to provide you with a name for you to call him. If you develop good rapport, he is apt to later give you a name.

Hopefully, in the meantime, you will uncover something to provide you with a positive ID. In the interest of time, and keeping the exercise moving along, it's good to have a strategy worked out for suspect identification. For example:

- One of the bank employees, who was able to escape, recognized him from earlier in the week; somehow, s/he can access notes to recover his name. (Maybe they can go to another branch of the bank to access the computers to pull it up)
- Someone who hears about the situation on the news, (maybe his parents), calls the police, because they think it might be their son.
- A vehicle search turns up item that leads to something else that leads to something else (For example, a restaurant receipt leads to a phone call asking if anyone knows a male of "x description," and you are told that he comes in often, and I think his first name is . . .)

Don't just "give" the negotiators this info. Make them work without it for a while, and more importantly, make them work to develop ideas to find out this information.

Daryl has a long history of street crime. He is of X ethnic descent. Depending on the familiarity of the role player of different sub-cultures, Daryl should be played true to that sub-cultural group: the more slang—if accurate and true-to-life—the better. It will be even better the slang is so heavy or confusing that the negotiator has to ask what the hostage taker is saying.

Initially, you will present as agitated and enraged. You have a history of several felony convictions and you claim you will not accept a third strike.

You will make typical demands, issue typical ultimatums regarding food and other items. One or two hostages will be released, if the negotiators do their job correctly.

28 – The Incident

Daryl selected a small branch bank close to a major highway. Generally speaking, three tellers and one manager work in this entire bank. It has been robbed several times before—its size and location making it ideal for the purpose. However, because of these previous robberies, the police have attempted to route patrols frequently in the area, and when Daryl presented his note to the teller, the teller pressed an emergency button, and nearby police arrived. Daryl spotted the cars approaching, ran to the entrance, and locked the door. Police could see Daryl brandishing his weapon, a Tec-9, at the four bank employees.

A megaphone is used to establish initial contact, and Daryl is urged to pick up the phone, which he does. Standard procedures are followed to cut all other phone lines, etc. Daryl can only talk to the police. (Of course, nowadays we have to worry if Daryl has a cell phone)

All in all, this seems like a typical hostage situation, following a typical trajectory of agitation, stabilization, and negotiation.

Then things will get stuck—Daryl will become increasingly belligerent and provocative, and he will seem unwilling to negotiate any further. He will not push it so far that SWAT must enter, but you are getting nowhere.

28 – Interview with Brother – Notes for the Role Player

The brother is initially hostile. He should push the interviewer's buttons, with claims of prejudice (based on whatever ethnic or religious group Daryl is playing). The interviewer will have to establish some mutual respect, or he will hang up the phone. If this happens, a 2ⁿᵈ negotiator better get on the phone and apologize.

If the interviewer doesn't approach the brother correctly, you won't get the info. Come on hard, and he'll hang up the phone on you.

A good exercise would be to have the brother dislike the one negotiator he talks to first (cause the negotiator's a man, cause she's woman, cause he/she has a dialect, etc.) Go with it for a while, to give the first negotiator some practice in dealing with a hostile interviewee…then, allow a switch—not because the brother demands it, but for your own reason (whatever you come up with)—and maybe the brother likes this negotiator better, and becomes more forthcoming with information.

What the Interviewer should be asking—but will not get unless s/he asks
Among the other questions, the interviewers are concerned, due to the current stasis, that Daryl might have a suicide-by-cop agenda. S/he should ask about such things as substance abuse and if he's made any previous suicide attempts.

The brother will be suspicious. The interviewer should explain that Daryl has let out a couple of hostages, and although it's bad, no one's been hurt. However, he's not made any demands, and you are afraid that Daryl may not want to come out of this alive. You are trying to get the hostages and Daryl out and safe.

Among the information that the brother knows is:
Daryl made a suicide attempt three weeks ago. He says, "Daryl got out of prison with his hopes high. He got a welding license in prison, but every time he goes to get a job, they ask where he got the license, and once they find out it was in prison, that's it. 'See yah.' So he did get some jobs working a door at the dance club on Broadway, the one that had the shooting a while back? So Daryl does his job, but that means getting in people's faces, and they get back in his. He's been in fights almost every night—it's that kind of place. So he threw out this guy last month; he was grabbing at girls' bodies and such. He kind of

lumped him up a bit, but the guy wouldn't leave. Instead, he spit in Daryl's face, and Daryl busted him up good. The man got what he deserved.

Problem is, the guy he threw out is the son of the deputy mayor. I don't mean any disrespect or anything to you people, but the police started coming around a lot after that. Seems too much to be a coincidence. So the bar fired him, said he was hurting business. So now he's got no job, he's got two kids from two mom's that he *wants* to support, and it's killing him. All I'm saying is he's been on edge a long time. I walked in on him the other night and he had the gun in his mouth and his finger on the trigger. He was crying and he looks at me and says, 'I can't do it. I don't have the stones to do it.'

Tell you the truth, I don't know if he expected to get away with this thing he's done."

Alternative Routes for the Role-Play
1. Daryl can get increasingly agitated and violent towards the remaining hostages, either necessitating excellent work on the part of the negotiator to keep him calm.
2. Entry by the SWAT team. This could be set up with all kinds of different tactical challenges.
3. Daryl can remain relatively calm, but the threat of suicide-by-cop will hang over the situation like an ominous cloud. The negotiator will have to determine how best to assess suicidal intent (the team leader can decide beforehand if the role player *should* be suicidal or not), and then, based on the assessment, how best to intervene.

---

28 – Psychological Consult

You need an "access route," a way to talk with Daryl that means something to him. The first access route is life itself. The longer you are talking: paraphrasing and dialoguing, the more connection you will establish. Human connection makes suicidal people think of life.

Beyond this, you need to understand Daryl's motivation for suicide, which will be based on his code of living.
1. If it is honor, try to wedge out the hostages, because "whatever else, they shouldn't be a part of what might happen."
2. If it is revenge on the system—the cops, who, as he sees it, are working for the mayor, tell him what he's said is public now. It's a matter of record, and IF he's telling the truth, then it's wrong. Dying won't fix things, and if any officers took part, "they certainly will get the consequences of such actions." "If what you are saying is true—no, I'm not calling you a liar, I just don't know, so let me continue—if what you are saying is true, that's the kind of thing that needs to be fixed."
3. If he is afraid of prison, you cannot pretend he won't be going back. Steer the conversation away from the realities of that, but don't pretend. You must find out why he's afraid of going back to prison—being caged, danger of other inmates, etc., before you can work with him about it.

4. If he simply is afraid to kill himself, or so he says, steer him away from talking about fear. Rather than not having enough courage to kill himself, get him to see that by staying alive, he is showing he has enough courage to live, as tough as things are right now. If possible, begin talking about his brother, his children and if he expresses love for them, begin to talk more about them, and how, despite his pain, they need him in this world. However, do not guilt trip him—rather, in the process of talking about them, you hope to have him realize that they need him in the world.

SCENARIO 28 – Checklist for After Action Review

The after action assessment/critique will depend on what was expressed and expected of the team going into the exercise. In other words, what was the desired training goal or outcome? Not just the outcome of the scenario, but what are the skills the director (team leader) is hoping to see exercised by the team, as these scenarios/situations develop?

Floor plan developed
- ❏ Did not meet goal
- ❏ Partially met goal
- ❏ Fully met goal

Demonstrate good listening skills
- ❏ Did not meet goal
- ❏ Partially met goal
- ❏ Fully met goal

Intel was able to ID subject in a timely manner
- ❏ Did not meet goal
- ❏ Partially met goal
- ❏ Fully met goal

Primary (team) was able to offer the subject "options" when discussing resolution
Cooperative effort worked out with local FBI HNT/agents
- ❏ Did not meet goal
- ❏ Partially met goal
- ❏ Fully met goal

SCENARIO 29

Footballus Interruptus (Negotiating with a Child)

29 – Original Call

Shots fired. Neighbors report hearing shots next door. They see three females, an adult and two adolescents, who have left the house in question and are out on the street.

Officers respond and talk with the three females: There's been some kind of family conflict. A teenage son has knocked out his father with a piece of firewood, fired several rounds from a handgun, hitting no one. Mother and teenaged daughters have run out of the house, and the youth is alone with his father.

Officers contain the house, and request SWAT and HNT.

29 – Interview with Mother and Daughters (Material for Role Players)

This should be made challenging for the interviewers. Do you separate all three, talk to them together or talk to the girls together and the mom separately?

The girls are going to be hyperventilating and hysterical, and they will interrupt each other. Mom will present as bitter, blaming and put upon, negative towards the police, towards her daughters, her son and towards her husband, Jimmy, but tending to excuse the latter. Getting information from her will be like pulling teeth; the only control she has in her life is making other people unhappy.

Jimmy Galeone, the father, is crazy for college football, so much so his family says there are two 'Jimmys'—there is the family man/working man/husband, but there is also the "Shut-the-fuck-up, I'm watching the game" Jimmy. He's bedrock Republican, very politically conservative and even a little racist, but he voted for Barack Obama because the democratic candidate alluded to using the office of president to have an actual national championship game. When his Republican friends objected, Jimmy responded, "Fuck the country. I mean it. Fuck the economy, fuck Iraq, fuck global warming or cooling or whatever. It's about time we got this football thing straightened out."

There is a history of domestic violence. When his team loses, he breaks things. When someone in the family makes a noise or distracts him, he tends to get physical. Fifteen years ago, he got so enraged at the baby crying that he grabbed him out of his wife's arms and shook him. He was incarcerated several years, took domestic violence prevention classes, which he passed with flying colors, (according to the therapist), and after several years of 'reconciliation therapy,' was reunited with his family.

His son, Angelo, aged fifteen, suffered brain damage from the shaking. He has always had difficulty in school, and has very poor impulse control. He's never been arrested, but he frequently gets detention and has a treatment aide to steer him around the school so he doesn't get in trouble. His two daughters, Junie and Christina, are quiet teenagers—they describe their lives as 'walking on eggs' for half the year (football season), and normal the rest. Jimmy's wife is an enabler—tells the kids to "Just keep out of your father's way. Let him watch his games—he works hard for this family and has a right to relax."

Today is a 'bowl weekend.' There are back-to-back games. Junie, who is sixteen, has not been allowed to date, but got invited out for the first time by a very nice kid, whose parents made an effort to call Mrs. Galeone, and introduce themselves. Every time Junie has tried to get permission from her father, he has just waved her off; he's too busy with the game(s). It's Saturday, the hopeful boyfriend has called several times whether he should buy the concert tickets—at $60 a non-refundable ticket, he doesn't want to buy them and not be able to go. Junie, after sixteen years of being treated like a nuisance, finally and unfortunately, got fed up. There are sixteen seconds left in the game, Jimmy's team down by five and the quarterback is back to pass for a touchdown or a loss. Junie, after the third time of hearing "Shaddup! Later! You're fucking blocking my view," yanked the cord out of the socket just as the pass was in the air.

Jimmy went ballistic and punched her in the face. Angelo, who has always been scared of his father and protective of his sisters at the same time, grabbed a log from the fireplace and knocked his father unconscious. Angelo ran and grabbed a gun from his father's nightstand, fired a round into the TV and screamed at his mother and sisters to "Get out!" They tried to calm him down, but he fired a second round past his mother's face. As far as Angelo is concerned, his mom has sold him out for years.

As they run out of the house, Angelo screams after them there are "going to be some changes around here."

29 – Planning for Practice – Different Alternatives for the Actual Negotiation

> ### On Scenarios Involving Children's Characters
> This role-play—and many others—will be too raw for a real kid, so either a high voiced adult or a tape of someone crying and asking to leave should be played in the background. If it's going to be verbally heard and not visually observed, often a female voice works well for an adolescent male. If you have exceptionally 'young acting' students at a college level, they can be suitable.

A team could certainly play the negotiation as a <u>simple one</u>. In that case, Jimmy remains unconscious, and Angelo is played as an agitated, frantic, impulsive kid, who is afraid of what's going to happen to him, both legally and when his father wakes up, and enraged at his father and wanting to kill him.

A more <u>complex negotiation</u> could include Jimmy, awake, furious and yelling, either in the background, distracting and further enraging his son, or actually on the phone as well. Angelo would play as in the first paragraph, and Jimmy simply makes things worse—as the negotiators try to calm him down, his response is his typical profanity and blame—it is very likely in a short time the negotiator will want to hit him upside the head as well.

Angelo's demands, at first incoherent, will center around a better home, where dad either moves out or changes the way he acts. He wants no more violence, no more yelling, and no more mom taking dad's side against the girls and him.

29 – Psychological Consult

FIRST CONTACT WITH ANGELO—RAPPORT BUILDING

Once you get Angelo somewhat calm, frame the situation as 'something bad enough has happened so the world finally knows how bad it is in the house.' He may be frantic or simply furious. The goal is assisting him in calming down. This may take considerable time. You have to communicate through your voice and what you say, that Angelo (and you) have all the time you need to make this work out safely. Angelo needs to believe you are on his side. Take all the time you need to accomplish this.

WARNING! Brain injuries and impulse control

Angelo has a chronic brain injury. If you speak too fast, use too big words, or complicated ideas, he will get confused. He will interpret this as you "making him stupid," and he will escalate. If you push him to act, or in any way, appear to demand that he "hurry up," he may feel overwhelmed and do something impulsive to get back in control. Because of his impulsiveness, he will be very dangerous. He could simply shoot his father on an impulse.

TACTICAL COMMUNICATION WITH THE FATHER

Once Angelo is calm—or if, due to the father's yelling, etc., Angelo is too distracted to communicate well with you—ask to speak to the father. He will be a loud, domineering ass. In a matter-of-fact tone, tell him he's got to quiet down. He'll focus on the football game. TELL HIM THE SCORE. <u>Guarantee the moment this is resolved, you'll have a taped replay of the last minute of play, if-and-only-if he shuts up and let's the negotiator do his job.</u> Emphasize to him that Angelo may kill him, if you, the negotiator, can't find a way to calm him down. He'll not only deny it, but will yell at Angelo, calling him a punk and a fucking whack job. At this point, there should be shouting and cursing between the role players, and it will be difficult (not impossible) for the negotiator to de-escalate the situation.

Point out Angelo's got a head injury, and that makes him very unpredictable and hard to control. Highlight the difficulties the school has with him, and what happened today. Firmly reiterate he now must let the police do their job by being silent. Tell him that he must not try to help by interjecting things, or demanding the phone. "From what your wife tells us, you know football as well as anyone alive. I wouldn't presume to disagree with you about what you know. Well, this is what I know, so let me do my job."

BACK TO ANGELO

Emphasize that changes in this home are going to happen—they have to, because of what has happened today. But those changes will only be good for his sisters (and him) if Angelo comes out with his father alive. Remind him he is a minor, so the courts are usually lenient, particularly when there is a conflicted or abusive family.

Beyond that, emphasize he clearly has been thinking of his sisters. They need their brother in this world, not locked away for a murder. Help him be protective for his sisters. Use the word "control" a fair amount. He's in control now and because of his control, he'll be able to help his sisters, releasing his father and coming out from the house, so "we all can get started in helping them."

Given the issue of control, do not use the word "surrender" when you are setting up how Angelo should emerge from the house. Rather, use something like, "To work this out, we have to do the following things. . . " Give him instructions on how to make that happen.

SCENARIO 29 – Checklist for After Action Review

The after action assessment/critique will depend on what was expressed and expected of the team going into the exercise. In other words, what was the desired training goal or outcome? Not just the outcome of the scenario, but what are the skills the director (team leader) is hoping to see exercised by the team, as these scenarios/situations develop?

Floor plan developed
- ❏ Did not meet goal
- ❏ Partially met goal
- ❏ Fully met goal

Demonstrate good listening skills
- ❏ Did not meet goal
- ❏ Partially met goal
- ❏ Fully met goal

Team developed a strategy for dealing with a teenager
- ❏ Did not meet goal
- ❏ Partially met goal
- ❏ Fully met goal

Child psych consultant considered?
- ❏ Did not meet goal
- ❏ Partially met goal
- ❏ Fully met goal

Specialized youth detective?
- ❏ Did not meet goal
- ❏ Partially met goal
- ❏ Fully met goal

What other ideas did Intel come up with to assist the young subject in coming to the right conclusion/resolution today?
- ❏ Did not meet goal
- ❏ Partially met goal
- ❏ Fully met goal

SCENARIO 30

Child Hostage Taker

30 – Original call

Caller on the phone with 9-1-1, stating he just shot his parents. Officers responded, contained the house, asked communications to have the caller come outside, and he refused. When police approach the house, Darren shoots through the door, and yelled, "I just want to die. Leave me alone and let me do it. I shot my mom and my dad! Leave me alone!"

A perimeter is set up and phone contact is made.

Officers requested SWAT and HNT.

If the available role player is female, choose a girl's name. It is far more likely that a boy would shoot his parents in such circumstances, but either can be made plausible.

On Scenarios Involving Children's Characters

This role-play—and many others—will be too raw for a real kid, so either a high voiced adult or a tape of someone crying and asking to leave should be played in the background. If it's going to be verbally heard and not visually observed, often a female voice works well for an adolescent male. If you have exceptionally 'young acting' students at a college level, they can be suitable.

---

30 – Information from 9-1-1 Call-taker who Spoke with Darren

9-1-1 received a call from Darren. He was sobbing and said: "I think I did something bad." He told the 9-1-1 call-taker he had shot his father and his mother with his father's gun. Darren said, "They beat me too much. She would hold me down and he would hit me. She used to make fun of me when I cried. So this time I made them stop."

30 – Scenario Alternative ONE

Darren shot each of his parents in the head. When asked if they were alive, he said he could see the inside of their heads. "I know they are dead. I'm next." The operator heard Darren ratchet back the slide of the gun, and she yelled at him to stop. Hurriedly speaking, she urged him to not take his life, doing the best she could to instill some sense he could come out of this awful situation. Darren screamed at her to leave him alone, and slammed down the phone.

<u>In this case, you will be simply trying to get a tragically distraught kid to surrender.</u>

30 – Scenario Alternative TWO

Darren shot each of his parents in the back. When asked if they were alive, he said he could see them breathing. "My dad is crying, but he can't get off the floor. My mom is cursing me out." The operator heard Darren ratchet back the slide of the gun, and she yelled at him to stop. Hurriedly speaking, she urged him to not shoot again, doing the best she could to instill some sense he could come out of this awful situation O.K. Darren screamed at her to leave him alone, and slammed down the phone.

<u>In this case, you will be trying to get a tragically distraught kid to surrender, but in addition, you have the pressure of time, of two wounded individuals, and how they may be distracting him, etc.</u>

30 – For the Director

Identification is probably not going to be a factor. Usually perpetrators like this, who commit a violent act and call 9-1-1 will answer all questions put to them by the 9-1-1-call taker. Furthermore, in this case, of course, you have the family members to speak with.

While the coach is working with the 9-1-1 call-taker (and additional HNT members, if possible), other HNT members can be working to set up and establish a NOC (negotiators operations center) near the command post, and start preparing for a possible transition.

If the situation is not resolved in a reasonable amount of time, and the team leader or scene commander makes the decision to do the transition, steps can then be taken to prepare the subject for the change in negotiators, as well as possible temporary loss of the communications if the technical patch doesn't work correctly. Be sure to have call back numbers, etc, at the ready, and prepare the subject in case something happens to the communications link.

Involving 9-1-1

This is an excellent scenario in which to involve your 9-1-1 call takers. Many police 9-1-1 telecommunications are requesting more training in crisis intervention cases, particularly those who transition into SWAT/HNT calls.

A scenario like this one, provides the perfect opportunity to begin the exercise with having the perpetrator make the call to 9-1-1 (mock, of course), and having a call taker playing themselves, take the call, and engage with this subject. The call taker should be required to gather the needed information, determine what is a necessary response to the call, (in smaller agencies, they would do the actual dispatch, as well), and keep this caller engaged while police respond.

Depending on the policies of the department, this call taker might be tasked with keeping this caller on the line until HNT is prepared to take over the call via a 'patch over,' if the department has that ability. Performing a transition and a technical patch over from a 9-1-1 call-taker to an HNT member is something that should definitely be practiced.

Another suggestion is for the team leader to determine if the 9-1-1 call-taker has established valuable rapport with the subject. If they have, the team leader might choose to keep that rapport for a while, and place a senior HNT member as 'coach' along side the 9-1-1 call-taker, at least in the early stages. This allows HNT to actually begin involvement in the call much sooner, with much less interruption to the caller.

30 – Interview with Child Protective Services

Child Protective Services have been intermittently involved with the Marx home for many years. There have been allegations of physical abuse on Darren Marx, aged eleven. Findings have been either unfounded or 'inconclusive.' Darren has alluded to beatings, but has always remained silent when formally interviewed. His mother and father have always denied any abusive actions, expressing disdain and outrage at CPS interventions.

30 – For the Director and Role Player

This will be a rather difficult scenario to effectively carry through. You will need a role player who can realistically play a pre-teen or teen. Perhaps the best would be a therapist who specializes in working with traumatized kids, who has some ability to act, probably a woman, as females tend to have voices at a higher register. At minimum, you should have a consultant who is familiar with children in crisis. The child will be emotionally labile, in other words, s/he will be anxious, scared, angry, defiant, sad, ingratiating. Rather than scripting all the nuances of such a child for an untutored role-player, you will need a child mental health professional who has an understanding of abuse, the damage it can inflict on a child and how such a child will think. The role player's task will be to stay in character—he (or she, as the case may be) will make no demands. Rather he will feel trapped by his circumstances, by what he has done and who he is. The negotiator's voice, his or her confidence and reassurance, is the lifeline to lead the child to surrender.

The role-player should prepare a story of abuse, both physical and sexual, that will both horrify and enrage the negotiator, and tug on the heartstrings as well. In short, a negotiator can lose perspective not just from adrenaline, from getting his or her buttons pushed and losing his or her temper, but out of sympathy as well.

This role-play, in particular, should have a time limit (the negotiators will not know it), as a role player may not know how to get the child to a place of surrendering naturally. The director, at this point, in a 'shadow role,' can walk them through the steps to surrender.

30 – Psychological Consultation

Whenever you do not have something significant to say, PARAPHRASE. Sum up your <u>understanding</u> of what the child has said (do NOT just mimic/mirror what they say). Your major task is to talk to this distraught child honestly and compassionately, without making your voice overly sweet. You must become the strength this child has always felt he lacked.

When he expresses anger at the negotiator, he is, in essence saying, "Where were you when I really needed you?" Express outrage, within limits, on his behalf. State if you had ever seen his parents do what Darren is describing, you would have stopped them. State how much you wish you had been there to catch them in the act of doing those terrible things.

Redirect (using either paraphrasing or kind, but firm direction), to talking about him, how people are here to help him, that he's been through a terrible time and he has survived it, and everyone here is going to help, each in their own way, to make his life better.

SCENARIO 30 – Checklist for After Action Review

The after action assessment/critique will depend on what was expressed and expected of the team going into the exercise. In other words, what was the desired training goal or outcome? Not just the outcome of the scenario, but what are the skills the director (team leader) is hoping to see exercised by the team, as these scenarios/situations develop?

Floor plan developed
- ❏ Did not meet goal
- ❏ Partially met goal
- ❏ Fully met goal

Demonstrate good listening skills
- ❏ Did not meet goal
- ❏ Partially met goal
- ❏ Fully met goal

Paraphrasing is really important with this subject
- ❏ Did not meet goal
- ❏ Partially met goal
- ❏ Fully met goal

Did team request assistance from adolescent psych consultant/specialist
- ❏ Did not meet goal
- ❏ Partially met goal
- ❏ Fully met goal

ABOUT THE AUTHORS

Ellis Amdur

Edgework founder Ellis Amdur received his B.A. in psychology from Yale University in 1974 and his M.A. in psychology from Seattle University in 1990. He is both a National Certified Counselor and a State Certified Child Mental Health Specialist. He has written a series of ten of books (many with subject-matter co-authors) concerning communication with mentally ill and emotionally disturbed individuals and the de-escalation of aggression.

Since the late 1960s, Amdur has trained in various martial arts systems, spending thirteen of these years studying in Japan. He is a recognized expert in classical and modern Japanese martial traditions and has authored three iconoclastic books and one instructional DVD on martial arts subjects.

Since his return to America in 1988, Ellis Amdur has worked in the field of crisis intervention. He has developed a range of training and consultation services, as well as a unique style of assessment and psychotherapy. These are based on a combination of phenomenological psychology and the underlying philosophical premises of classical Japanese martial traditions. Amdur's professional philosophy can best be summed up in this idea: "The development of an individual's integrity and dignity is the paramount virtue. This can only occur when people live courageously, regardless of their circumstances, and take responsibility for their roles in making the changes they desire."

Ellis Amdur is a pioneer in the Pacific Northwest concerning law enforcement training in de-escalating mentally ill and emotionally disturbed individuals. He attended the FBI's basic crisis negotiation course and has served as a consultant to a number of negotiation teams in hostage situations. He originally developed many of the role-plays in this book as crisis negotiation exercises, where he played the role of the hostage taker or person in crisis.

Ellis Amdur is a dynamic public speaker and trainer who presents his work throughout the U.S. and internationally. He is noted for his sometimes outrageous humor as well as his profound breadth of knowledge. His vivid descriptions of aggressive and mentally ill people and his true-to-life role-playing of the behaviors in question give participants an almost first-hand experience of facing the real individuals in question.

For more information on books and training by Ellis Amdur, please refer to his website at www.edgework.info

Biography of Ret. Sgt. Lisbeth Eddy

Lis obtained a BA in Speech-Communications from the University of Washington. She was hired by the Seattle Police department as an officer in 1979. She retired after thirty-one years of service. As a police officer, she worked over 10 years in the patrol division, as well as working as an officer-dispatcher in the communications division.

In 1988 Lis was assigned to the basic training division, where she taught Criminal Law. In 1992, Lis was promoted, and went back to patrol as a sergeant. In addition to being a patrol supervisor, and a Community Policing Team supervisor, she served in the Internal Investigations Division and as a Detective Sergeant in the Domestic Violence Unit.

In addition to these regular assigned duties, Lis was a member of the Hostage Negotiations Team, since 1981, and became the team leader in 1992. As a Hostage Negotiator, Lis has been involved in numerous incidents involving persons in crisis. She has attended basic and advanced hostage negotiators school, in addition to annual training seminars in negotiating crisis situations. Lis was selected to attend the two-week Crisis Negotiations School, sponsored by the FBI in Quantico, VA.

To increase her skills in communication with those in crisis, Lis worked over six years as a volunteer phone worker for the King County Crisis Clinic, eventually being asked to serve on their board of trustees.

Because of her involvement with the Hostage Negotiations Team, and her experience in dealing with persons in crisis, Lis was chosen to be a member of the committee that developed and implemented the Crisis Intervention Team (CIT) program on the Seattle Police Department in 1997. This unit trains officers on suggestions and options to use when encountering persons who are in crisis due to emotional disturbance or mental illness. Lis was selected to be the CIT coordinator in January of 2000. As a result of this involvement, Lis developed a strong partnership with the National Advocates for the Mentally Ill (NAMI) to explore a better response for law enforcement in dealing with mentally ill individuals. In 2002, Lis received the Jefferson Award for her contributions to the community in working to assist mentally ill persons to reduce their involvement with the police, and ensure their safety, and the safety of the community. She was recognized in 2003 by Good Housekeeping magazine, as one of the recipients of their annual Women in Government awards.

Most recently, she has served as a consultant to the Washington State Criminal Justice Training Commission to assist in the development and implementation of the CIT training for all law enforcement officers in King County.

Lis is considered to be a nationally recognized expert on issues involving police response to dealing with the mentally ill. She has participated in national panels exploring best practices (PERF) involving police interactions with both mentally ill individuals as well as working effectively with the mental health system. She has been consulted as a subject matter expert the United States Department of Justice concerning the effective utilization of resources in setting up CIT programs. Lis has participated internationally, as well, having presented at Police/Mental Health conferences in England and Australia.

CPSIA information can be obtained
at www.ICGtesting.com
Printed in the USA
LVHW022010190723
752945LV00007B/37